HUMOROUS SKITS FOR YOUNG PEOPLE

Humorous Skits
for
Young People

*A collection of royalty-free short plays
and easy-to-perform comedy sketches*

By

Robert Fontaine

Publishers   **PLAYS, Inc.**   *Boston*

PN
6120
.A5
F523

Library of Congress Catalog Card Number: 65-22677
ISBN: 0-8238-0023-7

CONTENTS

HUMOROUS SKITS FOR YOUNG PEOPLE

THE EFFICIENCY EXPERT

The setting of this skit is the National Widget & Gizmo Co., as a sign might say without fear of contradiction. Chairs and desks are included in the set—everything should be nice and cozy. There must be a large chart on the wall, showing profits rising steadily.

❖ ❖ ❖ ❖ ❖

Characters

THE BOSS, *a nice chap who has mother-in-law trouble*

GEORGE, *an honest worker*

BELLE, *one more honest worker*

BRENDA, *still another*

MARY, *and another*

PAUL, *and one more, who, like the others, enjoys work except when he can avoid it*

LANCELOT, *a young efficiency expert loved by nobody but himself*

AT RISE: BELLE, BRENDA *and* GEORGE *are sitting around, relaxing.* GEORGE *gets up and goes to the chart.*

GEORGE: Well, the latest chart shows National Widget & Gizmo is still increasing its profits. (*He yawns and stretches his arms.*) Just a nice, slow, steady climb.

1

BELLE (*Lazily*): I'll bet the boss could double the profits if he really wanted to.

BRENDA: It wouldn't be fun, though. That's the nice thing about National Widget. People like to work here. No time clocks to punch. Two hours for lunch. Paid holidays for Arbor Day, First Day of Spring. . . .

GEORGE: No push. No rush. No cafeteria where you have to run back to work with your veal cutlet and boiled potato in your hands after twenty minutes.

BRENDA: Six weeks' paid vacation.

GEORGE: We're all happy, contented workers here. That's why business keeps getting better and better. (MARY *and* PAUL *stroll in casually.* GEORGE *waves to them.*) Hi. Anyone want to play a little canasta?

PAUL: I'll play a while, although I really should be packing gizmos.

MARY: Deal me in. I'm supposed to be polishing widgets but I think there are enough done for one day.

BELLE: I'm going to take a nap . . . and if I wake up before quitting time, I might sort some gizmos. Depends on how I feel.

BRENDA: That's right. Take it easy. The boss always says no one should leave this plant tired. (BELLE *dozes off. Others begin to play cards.*)

PAUL (*To* GEORGE): Did you get out that order for American Gizmo in Buffalo?

GEORGE: I meant to, but I started reading a good detective story and I forgot all about it.

PAUL: Oh, well . . . you can get it off some time this spring.

BRENDA (*To* MARY): I guess we're the only people who still polish widgets by hand.

2

MARY: Everyone says hand-polished widgets are much better.

PAUL: Did anyone ever find out *what* a widget is?

MARY: I asked the boss once, and he said he had no idea; he took over the factory from his father.

BRENDA: Same with gizmos. People just order them and we send them.

PAUL (*Thoughtfully*): I wonder if the boss will be the same easy-going young fellow after he gets married.

MARY: Why not?

GEORGE: People change sometimes. (*The* Boss *walks in quietly. The others smile and nod.*)

Boss: I hope I'm not disturbing anyone.

BELLE (*Wakes up suddenly*): Oh, hello, boss.

Boss: I hope I didn't wake you up.

BELLE: No. It's almost quitting time. I'd hate to sleep on my *own* time.

Boss: If I'm not being too bold . . . I hope you all don't mind if I suggest you get out that big order of gizmos for Amalgamated Doohickey sometime. It's a *rush* order. But don't let that upset you. Anytime within the next few months.

PAUL: We'll see, boss.

Boss: I hate to bother you about it.

MARY: That's all right, boss. You have some rights, too.

Boss (*Thoughtfully—he is a little worried*): Yes. Uh . . . my . . . uh . . . mother-in-law-to-be . . . has a notion . . . ahem . . . well . . . she thinks things could be improved here.

GEORGE: The chairs could be reupholstered.

Boss: Yes. Uh . . . she asked me to take on a fellow . . . Lancelot . . . business administration expert . . . in fact he's due here any moment . . . hope you won't mind giving him a try. (*They all ad-lib "O.K., Why not?, Sure, boss," etc.*) Ah, here he is. (LANCELOT *comes in briskly, rubbing his hands together, smiling in a sickeningly assured fashion.*) This is Lancelot. (*Others start to speak or shake hands.*)

LANCELOT (*Pushing them all back and holding up his hands for silence*): Let's not waste time being friendly. I'm here for one purpose and one purpose only. Friends I can make any time. I'm here to put the spur to you people. We have to up production. We have to cut out the frills. I can see you are all happy and contented. Nothing could be worse. A happy worker is a sloppy worker. It's the worker who has every bit of energy whipped out of him who produces. Any questions? (*The workers start to speak but he doesn't wait.*) We don't have time for questions. My system is a simple one. While you are here you should be working, and while you are working you should be doing everything possible. For example, I have watched one of you packing widgets, using only one hand. The other hand was wasted, as were both legs and feet. I've all sorts of plans and systems worked out so there won't be a wasted motion. If you're wrapping widgets with one hand, you can be whipping cream with the other . . . you can be crushing grapes with your feet . . . things like that. Now, I want you all to come into my office, one by one, so I can make you forget you are lazy, inefficient human beings. You must realize you are cogs in a vast machine.

PAUL: Could I get a glass of water?

LANCELOT: From now on, all of you will drink a quart of water *before* you come to work. (*To* PAUL) All right, you can be the first into my office. The rest of you, get back to work! (*The workers stare at each other, stunned. The* Boss *hangs his head.* Lancelot *claps his hands impatiently.*)

CURTAIN

* * * *

Scene Two is some months later. Things have changed. The workers are still around but they are working: twisting things with their fingers, hammering, knocking things with their shoulders and heads, stamping things with their feet and looking, for all the world, as if they were doing a highly productive rain dance in Africa. A large chart on the wall now shows the profit line going down.. At one side there is a large sheet of paper labelled "Universal Magnificent Electronic Computer." There are five large circular holes in it.

George (*Working feverishly with hands, feet, etc., as are the others*): Look at that chart. (*He points toward chart and indicates profit line going down.*) That's what our new efficiency expert has done. We do five times as much work . . .

Mary: And we're losing money.

Paul: I told you the boss would change when he got married.

Belle: It's his mother-in-law. She's money-mad. Lancelot, the efficiency expert, is her cousin.

Brenda: Lancelot! I'll bet he sleeps at night with balloons attached to his nose . . . so he can blow them up while he snores.

George: I can't stand that guy. I had lunch with him in the cafeteria and he clocked himself. He ate soup, stew, des-

5

sert, and coffee in three minutes and eleven seconds. He said he cut four seconds from his record.

MARY: Not counting the bicarbonate.

PAUL: That time clock kills me. You punch in and a vitamin pops into your mouth.

MARY: I punched in late one day and I got an eraser.

BRENDA: The vitamins go off at 8:59.

GEORGE: You're lucky, Mary. They're installing a wooden plank . . . if you punch in after nine, it comes down and raps you on the head.

PAUL: And you can't punch out before five. If you do, it releases a catch and a dog comes out of a cage and snarls at you.

BRENDA: A very efficient dog. Lancelot has trained him to live on the string left over from tying up widgets. (*While they talk, remember, these workers are moving their hands and arms and legs, etc., apparently working on various assembly lines.*)

GEORGE (*Nods toward the computer*): That computer is the limit. Lancelot's been feeding it information for a week. Today's the day he gets a big, significant answer.

MARY: It'll probably suggest we polish widgets with our noses if he can get a belt to go by that high.

PAUL: Today's the day Lancelot is going to show the boss all the new operations we can do, too.

BELLE: Sh-h-h . . . here they come. (*Everyone works a little faster, casting nervous glances at the computer. LANCELOT strides in jauntily, followed by the Boss— now a pale, nervous and uneasy man.*)

LANCELOT (*Cockily rubbing hands together*): Here is where we have made the most improvement.

Boss (*Uneasily*): Yes. This is where everything was easy and casual. Of course, the profits *were* going up.

LANCELOT: Yes?

BOSS (*Wistfully*): And now they're going down.

LANCELOT: A temporary adjustment of the influx to the outgo. (*Pause*) I want to point out an example of the recovery of wasted motion—Belle. (BELLE *smiles wanly.*) You will notice that Belle is not merely wrapping widgets with her hands and placing gizmos on the belt with her knees, she is also squirting liquid wax with her feet, while the others dance about, polishing the floor.

BOSS (*Wearily*): That does save a lot of time. My mother-in-law is all for it, one hundred percent.

LANCELOT: Yes. A discerning woman. Now, you will notice that George, while he trims gizmos and paints widgets, also hops up and down every now and then, turning this butter churner.

BOSS: Butter churner?

LANCELOT (*Proudly*): Yes. An example of widening the variety of our products. We're selling butter now, too. (*Takes a step or two.* BOSS *follows, but looks nervously at the computer.*) Paul cuts the material into the proper size for molding king-size filtered widgets. While he is doing this . . . show the boss, Paul.

PAUL (*Reluctantly*): Over here, below . . . an assembly line of pecans, walnuts and peanuts comes by. (*Pantomimes*) As I cut the widget stuff here . . . I bang my head against the nuts and crack them . . . then I kick up my right knee and catch them in a bag . . . meanwhile knocking the shells on the floor with my left hip . . . as I do this I whirl around with a small vacuum cleaner attached to my waist . . . thus . . . and draw up the shells.

LANCELOT (*To* BOSS): Next week we are going to see if we can't stuff sofa pillows with them.

Boss (*Nervously, to* PAUL): You can slow down now.

PAUL: It takes a little time once I get started.

LANCELOT (*Looking at watch*): There's a lot more I could show you but it's time for the million-dollar computer to give us the information that will make our future brilliant and successful.

Boss (*A little sadly, to* BRENDA): You don't play cards any more, do you?

BRENDA: We wouldn't think of it.

LANCELOT: Don't distract them! They must work as the machines do. We are making machines out of them . . . happy, contented, efficient machines. And now, the computer's message! This machine will give us an answer that would have taken five hundred men three hundred years to arrive at.

Boss: What if it's the wrong answer?

LANCELOT (*Scornfully*): It can't be the wrong answer, not with memory banks, diamond feedbacks and three thousand transistors. This machine is *more* intelligent than the human brain. What it says is *truth* . . . and what it orders *must* be obeyed.

Boss: Sounds a little frightening to me.

LANCELOT (*Suddenly*): Wait! The answer is coming! (*Sounds are heard behind the computer: buzzes, singing, chatter, etc.*) Sounds almost human, doesn't it? (*While* LANCELOT *and the* Boss *are concentrating on the machine as if hypnotized, the workers have quietly sneaked behind it. Now their hands come out of the prepared holes. One pair has paper and pencil and is writing.*) It is beginning to reply. (*The paper is passed on to the next pair of hands which writes and passes it along. One hand shakes the hand of the next and the hands not doing anything are wiggling and making church-and-steeple or cat's cradle with fingers. Third hand passes paper along. The hands wiggle. The paper is marked and passed back and forth mysteriously, while singing, moaning and humming sounds go on.*) We should get the message soon. The memory banks and transistors are all working furiously. (*At length, the long strip of paper comes out of a hole and the* Boss *picks it up and reads it slowly as* LANCELOT *peers over his head.*)

Boss (*Reading slowly and clearly*): Get rid of that nutty efficiency expert before you go bankrupt. Fire him!!! (LANCELOT *looks over* Boss's *shoulder, terrified, then goes over close to the machine and bows as if it were a god.*)

LANCELOT: I bow to you, O great computer! (*Two hands come out of the holes and start to slap him. He backs away, scared. Another hand slaps the back of his head while still another comes down on top of his head. One now pulls out his necktie, another musses his hair. He finally goes running off wildly.*)

Boss (*Turns his back and reads more of the "message" as the workers tiptoe back to their jobs*): And get rid of that mother-in-law of yours. (*He smiles and reads further.*) You weigh 155 pounds and you will have good fortune if you give everybody a raise. (*He turns around. Workers are all smiling innocently.*) You will all get a ten percent raise and a fifty percent reduction in work. We have to get this place back to the old way . . . when we were making money and we were happy. (*The workers cheer. They assume the old casual, good-natured postures, except* PAUL, *who can't stop his motions. They hold him until he calms down.*)

9

BRENDA: Anyone for a game of cards?

GEORGE: You go ahead. I think I'll spend a few minutes taking the works out of the time clock.

BOSS: That's the spirit! (*Curtain.*)

THE END

LET SLEEPING BEAUTIES LIE

This is a story about a Prince Charming, a Sleeping Beauty, a Wizard, a King, and all that exciting and romantic stuff. You all know the traditional story, but you don't know the inside dope. This is it. The setting is a palace. If you don't have a palace, just put up a sign that says: Royal Palace: We Have Been in Business 300 Years. *The time is long, long, loooong ago. Afternoon.*

❖ ❖ ❖ ❖ ❖

Characters

King, *a bored king*
Jester, *a not-very-funny jester*
Prince Charming, *the king's son and heir*
Wizard, *a magic-worker who has seen his best days*
Dragon, *a retired dragon*
Sleeping Beauty, *a princess who has been asleep a thousand years (this part should be played by a boy)*

At Rise: *The* King *is sitting on a throne. His* Jester *sits at his feet. The* King *looks bored. He takes off his crown, looks at it, then puts it back on.*

King: I should put on my summer crown. It's after May 15th. (*He shifts about restlessly.*) Say something funny,

11

Jester. That's what I hired you for. Last month a jester was thrown in a dungeon and his head cut off.

JESTER: Did he have blue eyes and brown hair?

KING: No.

JESTER: Was he about five feet tall and about a hundred and twenty pounds?

KING: No.

JESTER: Was he about thirty years old?

KING: No.

JESTER: That's a relief, O King!

KING: Why?

JESTER: It *couldn't* have been *me*. (KING *glares at him.* PRINCE CHARMING *comes in.*)

PRINCE: Hi, King. Hi, Jester.

JESTER (*Bowing*): Hail to thee, Prince Charming.

KING: Why aren't you out slaying dragons or fighting in tournaments . . . or saving beautiful damsels in distress? All you do is hang around the palace, tied to your mother's ermine strings.

PRINCE: Saving damsels? That's for the birds. Have you looked over the crop of princesses? Real dogs. If I could find a really beautiful one to fight for, it would be different.

JESTER: Hast thou not heard of Sleeping Beauty?

PRINCE: Who?

JESTER: The most beautiful girl in the world. She lies sleeping and has been sleeping for a thousand years.

KING: Man! I'll bet she'll be stiff when she wakes up!

PRINCE (*To* JESTER): Tell me more, unworthy Jester.

JESTER: I just thought of something funny: A successful king is one who can collect more taxes than the queen can spend.

KING: Not very funny. Tell us more about Sleeping Beauty.

JESTER: The one who braves the dragon and the fierce magician and the other dangers that stand in the way . . . the man who does this, and awakens Sleeping Beauty with a kiss . . . will be her husband and rule over the largest kingdom in the world.

KING: Has this rumor been confirmed?

JESTER: Definitely. I saw it in the Queen's crystal ball in living color last week.

PRINCE (*Thoughtfully*): It sounds like a good deal.

KING: I get ten percent. (*He rubs his hands.*)

JESTER: I'm entitled to the oil rights, the fishing rights, and the dragon-broth concession.

KING (*Pointing off*): Go, my son, show your bravery! I'm getting sick of the whole kingdom telling me you're a weak-kneed nincompoop with the brain of a sparrow. You're not that bad, are you?

PRINCE: Even if I *am*, it isn't nice for our subjects to kid about it. (*Pause*) I will go. I will take Arthur's magic sword that has been in the family for years.

KING: It's an antique. Like your mother. Except the sword shuts up once in a while. Off you go, my boy. Good luck to you. If you have bad luck, you have eleven other brothers who will be glad to inherit my kingdom. So don't worry.

PRINCE (*To* JESTER): Which way is it?

JESTER (*Pointing off*): Toward Avalon and the Isles of Wonder. East of the sun and west of the moon. Go one mile down the road past the tournament grounds . . . turn left at the Gingerbread House . . . when you come to little Red Riding-Hood's grandmother's, you'll see a wolf who runs a hay market . . . a horse filling station. He'll give you a road map.

PRINCE: I'll put on my armor and go. I think I ought to

13

wear something drip-dry with a tab collar. Tally-ho! I'm off! (*He raises his arm and charges off.*)

CURTAIN
* * * *

Scene Two is a few days later. The setting is a woods with a cave at one side. The PRINCE *is wandering slowly about the stage, sword in hand. Finally, he sits down on a rock.*

PRINCE (*To himself*): Ah, well, lackaday! Hey nonny nonny. Tally-ho! and all that. I've been traveling for days and no sight have I seen of dangerous dragons or wicked wizards . . . never mind the beautiful Sleeping Beauty. I should have stood in bed . . . or loafed around the palace playing my gee-tar. I'm not such a bad guy. I'm not such a dope. If I had kept at it, I'd have been an Eagle Scout by now . . . with my own knots and everything. (WIZARD *enters. He should be dressed crazily with a wizard's hat, if possible, and certainly he should carry a wand.*)

WIZARD (*Waving wand*): I appear! Hail, Prince. From nowhere, in a twinkling, have I come. And to help you.

PRINCE: *That* I don't believe. (*Stands up quickly*) Stand aside or I shall have your head. (*He waves his sword.*)

WIZARD: Don't be silly. I have dozens of heads.

PRINCE (*Firmly*): One side. You want to stop me from finding Sleeping Beauty.

WIZARD (*Suddenly angry*): You shall *never* find her. I shall turn you into a frog.

PRINCE: Oh, come on! A frog! How silly can you get? How about a tiger? Or an eagle? Or a sports car with bucket seats?

14

WIZARD (*Impressively*): Hocus, pocus, omnia Gallia, semper fidelis, cha-cha-cha. (*He dances about, waving his wand around.*) O, sole mio, bubble, bubble, toil and trouble, heart of a lizard and gizzard of a wizard . . .

PRINCE (*Crooning*): I love you.

WIZARD (*Frowning*): You're no help. (*Pause*) Oh, invisible workers of the black world and dragons of the depths of the earth, give him . . . give him . . . give him. . . . (*He stops and shakes his head sadly.*)

PRINCE: You've had it.

WIZARD: I guess this just isn't my day. I'll change my way of life. I'll have to start on the health foods . . . wheat germ . . . high protein dragon meat and fresh unicorn horns. My wife warned me. (*Sighs*) You don't really want to wake up Sleeping Beauty, do you?

PRINCE: I have so sworn. (*He raises sword solemnly.*)

WIZARD (*Shrugs*): Well, it was written that he whom I could not cast my spell over . . . he must fight the dragon in yonder cave—(*Points dramatically*) and then *onward* . . . to Sleeping Beauty. (*Wistfully*) It will be a shame to awaken her after all these years. (*Pause*) Wackis, ruckus . . . hoop-dee-doo . . . ta-ra-ra boom-dee-ay! (*He walks out swiftly.*)

PRINCE: He's some kind of nut. (*He goes to cave.*) Hey, Dragon! You wanna fight? (*Pause*) Hey, Dragon! My father can lick your father. One, two, your mother's nose is blue, your father is a sleepyhead, just like you. Ha, ha, ha, ha. Knock this bronze medal off my shoulder.

DRAGON (*Poking head out of cave, and speaking in a tired voice*): Oh, go away. No one has bothered me in hundreds of years. I'm not used to all this fuss. I'm perfectly happy here with my transistor radio and my electric blanket. (*Disappears into cave*)

15

PRINCE: Fie! It is written that the dragon will help me to be happy when I awaken Sleeping Beauty. (DRAGON *pokes head out again.*)

DRAGON: You don't have to *fight* me for that. I'm not going to breathe fire or shake the earth or any of that stuff. You can *have* Sleeping Beauty. No one has claimed her in a thousand years. I'm just a tired old dragon who intends to be peaceful and happy. (*Returns to cave*)

PRINCE: Dragon! The king's astrologers insist you are important to this deal. Come out, come out, wherever you are! (*Dances around singing the last sentence*)

DRAGON (*Coming out*): Why do you annoy me? You won't want Sleeping Beauty when you get her. And you are *not* going to chop off my head because I happen to *need* it.

PRINCE (*Waving his sword*): Sorry, old pal, but I must have your head.

DRAGON: Wait! I'll give you something more valuable. (*Hands the* PRINCE *a scroll*) This scroll has a lifetime guarantee. If it does not work, send it back with five thousand gold pieces to cover postage and transportation. (*He goes back into cave.*)

PRINCE (*Unrolls scroll, reads aloud*): To whom it may concern, and this means *you*. In case of emergency, break seal and read scroll. This is the spell that will put Sleeping Beauty *back* to sleep. Say aloud, while dancing in a circle, "Oh, doch and doris, sleep-us snore-us!" (*He starts to throw scroll away*) Why would I want to put her to sleep again? (*Stops for a moment, thoughtfully.*) Oh, well . . . you never can tell. (*He tucks scroll under arm.*) On to Sleeping Beauty!

CURTAIN
* * * *

Scene Three takes place a few hours later, at another palace. At rise, SLEEPING BEAUTY *is fast asleep on the throne. The* PRINCE *comes in. He stops and stares. Then he smiles. He looks up at a sign that says:* DO YE NOTTE DISTURB. *He takes down the sign, leans over and kisses* SLEEPING BEAUTY. *She wakes up, rubs her eyes and then stands up.*

SLEEPING BEAUTY (*Annoyed*): You've come at last. Well, it took you long enough. Now you're my king and my husband, and you'll do what I tell you. The first thing . . . this place needs a good airing out. I want to change the drapes and curtains. We need new rugs . . . it *is* spring, isn't it? If it isn't, I'll order spring. Did you wipe the mud off your feet when you came in? You haven't shaved. Not since yesterday, I'll bet. Is that the best suit of armor you could find? It's too small around the waist. (*Moves around*) Look at the dust! You can write your name in it. Well, that's what you have to expect when the cleaning woman hasn't come in in a thousand years. Don't just stand there. (*Stares at scroll and at* PRINCE, *who is stunned by her chatter*) What's that?

PRINCE: A scroll. You see. . . .

SLEEPING BEAUTY: Well, you're not going to hang it up around here. It doesn't *go* with anything. Your room will be upstairs over the dungeon. You can put all your junk in there. And don't go asking all your relatives to come to visit us. They'll just sponge. (*Looks around*) That throne never looked right there. Here, help me move it. (SLEEPING BEAUTY *and* PRINCE *pick up throne. She lets him hold it, while she ponders.*) Over there. (*He lugs it.*) No. Over *there.* (*He lugs it.*) No, no. That won't do. Over there, temporarily. We'll move it some other time. (PRINCE *moves throne and sits down*) Get up!

17

That's *my* throne. Yours is a little, dinky one with gold-plated arms. (PRINCE *groans and rises.*)

PRINCE: I . . . well, frankly, this wasn't the way I thought it would turn out.

SLEEPING BEAUTY: I know. Romantic. Fairy-tale stuff. I suppose you thought you'd just sit around and do nothing all day . . . just loaf and eat grapes and dance and shoot owls. Well, let me tell you, you'll do no such thing. (*While she talks, he takes the scroll out, sighs, is thoughtful a moment, then shrugs. She points to scroll.*) What *is* that? That's no scroll. It's a letter from some rival, I'll bet. I know men. They like the noisy, pushy type. I'm not that way. I'm quiet and soft-spoken. You'll never hear me nagging, not unless I *have* to.

PRINCE (*Looking at scroll*): Oh, doch and doris, sleep-us, snore-us . . .

SLEEPING BEAUTY: Huh? (*She blinks and yawns.*)

PRINCE: In the name of thy king now long gone, who put you to sleep because you wouldn't shut-us up-us . . . I command thee . . . in the name of all the good fairies, elves, pixies, the Secretary of Labor, the Yankee first baseman and all other workers of white magic . . . to sleep-us . . . slumber-us . . . hocus, pocus. . . .

SLEEPING BEAUTY: But . . . (*Her eyes close. She yawns and stretches her arms.*)

PRINCE: Sleep-us-snore-us. (SLEEPING BEAUTY *moves back to the throne and goes to sleep, snoring. The* PRINCE *waits a moment to be sure she is asleep. He starts to tiptoe out, stops.*) Wow! *That* was a close call! (*Curtain*)

THE END

FAIR TODAY, FOLLOWED BY TOMORROW

If you have ever watched a TV weather forecast, you will be able to put your heart, soul and umbrella into this skit. It sometimes seems that the forecaster is deliberately trying to confuse you. Well, it wouldn't be surprising. The setting is a room at television station WUWU-TV in Boston, Massachusetts. There is a table with some chairs around it. It would be nice to have a big map of the United States, badly drawn, on a blackboard or a big white sheet of paper. Some slips of paper and black crayons would be helpful. The time is an evening in midwinter.

❖ ❖ ❖ ❖ ❖

Characters

JODHPUR COOPER, *head of WUWU-TV, who doesn't like the weather forecasts*

AGNES FLINCH, *his aide, who doesn't either*

HAROLD HARP, *News Chief of WUWU-TV, who wants more drama in the weather*

PETE RASKINS, *weather forecaster, who gets the message*

A STRANGER, *who saves the day*

AT RISE: JODHPUR COOPER *is seated at the head of the table. Around the table are seated* AGNES FLINCH, HAROLD

HARP, *and* PETE RASKINS. PETE *is a mild, affable, diffi-
dent fellow, who takes advice from everyone.*

JOD: Now, we have a few minutes before our fifteen-minute
weather forecast and I want to talk it over. We have a lot
of competition in Boston in weather forecasting. We
have to get this thing dramatized properly.

AGNES: My main complaint, as assistant to the Chief here,
is that we tell people the weather too quickly. Once they
know what the weather is going to be, they tune out. I'm
talking about the *local* weather.

HAROLD: As head of the news department of WUWU-TV,
I've noticed that. I've nothing against Pete here. He sells
the gas ranges and air conditioners very well. He makes
you *yearn* for them. It breaks your heart the way he begs
you to cook with gas. But how many people are left to
watch and listen if he gives the weather forecast right
away?

PETE: Well, I often tell them it's a bad drying day, first.
You know, this is pretty risky. I never did a wash in my
life. How do I know if it's a good drying day?

JOD: You get a dozen reports from the United States
weather bureaus all over the country.

PETE: But they're all conflicting.

AGNES: What do *they* know?

JOD (*Holding his hand over his heart and standing up*):
Just a moment, Agnes. You are talking about the United
States of America, land of my birth. What is good enough
for Uncle Sam is good enough for me. (*Sings*) "From sea
to shining sea . . ." (*He sits down, moved.*)

HAROLD: Remember, tonight is our thirty-day extended
forecast, *too.* We have to get together on that.

PETE: Well, I have a report from my grandmother upstate.

She says the woolly bear caterpillars are shedding. That means warm weather.

AGNES: My sister, downstate—she runs a guppy farm—says the guppies are hiding behind each other. That means a cold and windy month ahead.

HAROLD (*Picking up slip of paper*): I have a report here from the U-P-A-P-O-P Press that says in eastern Massachusetts the bald eagles are growing thick hair. This means a pretty cold time ahead.

JOD: There are *no* bald eagles around here.

AGNES: To me, that's all the more convincing.

PETE: Well, my uncle in Framingham has a parrot that keeps saying "Get an umbrella." That means a lot of snow or rain.

JOD (*Takes slip of paper*): I have a letter here from my mother in Concord. She says the moles are all digging wells. That means a pretty dry month. Concord, the very cradle of liberty, you know. My uncle, in Lexington, says the beagles are making holes in their kennels. This is a sure sign there'll be very little rain.

PETE: Well, I guess we have an all-around picture of the weather for the next thirty days, so the extended forecast won't be hard.

JOD: No, it's the day-to-day stuff we have to work on. (*He gets up and goes to map. He draws any old kind of line or squiggle with points on it or something.*) Here, in the northwest quadrant, is where we should start. Oregon has a weak low, a strong high, and a weak middle. It looks like a small blizzard. (*He turns up his collar, pretends to skate and starts singing*) "Jingle bells, jingle bells . . ." Now, down here in California and Arizona and all those faraway places . . . (*He makes more silly squiggles and draws a face. Then he goes to table and takes paper from* PETE.) Down here there's a south-south-west wind, shifting to an east wind off the Pacific. (*Draws a cloud with a mouth blowing*)

PETE: Excuse me, boss, how can an east wind blow into California off the Pacific?

JOD: That's *your* job.

AGNES (*To* JOD): The world is round, isn't it?

PETE: Most places I've been, it was flat.

HAROLD (*To* PETE): Well, it's round. I know a fellow who can prove it. The east wind is blowing right around the world into San Diego.

JOD: Pay attention, Pete. I'm showing you how to delay the *local* weather. Now here in the Midwest, there's a high moving *down* from Canada. You can tell because it has a new Canadian flag on it. Moving *up* from Alabama is a low-pressure area that will meet the high-pressure area in Duluth, Minnesota, on Saturday afternoon at three o'clock and cause heavy rain, heavy dew, gusts of wind up to sixty miles an hour and a lot of wet feet.

PETE: I think I'm getting the idea, sir. Could I try?

JOD: Good. Certainly. (PETE *goes up to map.*)

PETE: Winston-Salem, North Carolina, will have smoky weather as will lower Kentucky. Thus it will be a good day for smoking hams.

AGNES: Very good, Pete. We're still nowhere *near* the Boston weather.

PETE (*Looking at papers*): From the United States Weather Bureau there are warnings of winds of hurricane force. (*He stops, puts up his hands as if to protect himself, turns his head into the wind, tries manfully to walk against it.*)

HAROLD: Nice going, Pete.

PETE: This will be about fifty miles off the coast of Louisiana. In Washington there will be a lot of hot air rising as debate continues in Congress. This will run smack into a cold front from the Gulf of Mexico, and heavy rains will fall. (PETE *pretends to put up an umbrella and hold it.*) Heavy rains. In northern Florida the heat wave will continue. (*He puts down umbrella and pretends to dive into the ocean, then swims about for a moment.*)

JOD: Fine, fine! We still could never *guess* what the weather is in Boston.

PETE (*Stops swimming*): In Pennsylvania, there is a chance of freezing rain. (*He pretends to slip and grabs a chair, making his way cautiously back to map.*) Freezing rain and sleet. Motorists are advised to start their cars backwards as they're going to skid around anyway. In New Orleans, gentle, spring-like weather will prevail, with quiet zephyrs and light blue skies. (PETE *dances around, playing pipes and then humming "Spring Song." He goes back to the board.*)

JOD: Splendid, Pete. You'll be on the air in a minute or two and I think you'd better shorten this. Of course you can go on and on—when you're on the air. Tell them the temperature in Moscow. Tell them what's going to happen tomorrow in London.

AGNES: Let them know what's happening in South America —storms and earthquakes and all.

HAROLD: Give them the temperatures and humidity in the jungles of Africa.

JOD: O.K., that's enough. Now, give them the local weather.

PETE (*Looking through a lot of papers*): I don't think I *have* a local forecast. Dear, dear! (*He continues to look through papers. So does everybody else*)

JOD (*Holding up paper*): What's this? (*Reading*) "Much colder followed by about two inches of snow."

PETE: That's from last January. I just keep them for my scrapbook. (*He continues to look.*)

AGNES: Why don't we just look out the window? (PETE *rushes to what is supposed to be a window. He presses his face against it.*)

JOD: Is it sunny?

PETE: I can't tell. It's too foggy.

HAROLD: I don't mind holding up the local weather to the *end,* but we have to give it to the viewers sometime. And I don't mean last *January's* forecast, either. (*A* STRANGER *comes in the door, with dripping umbrella, wet, dripping raincoat, face all wet, wringing water out of his hat.*)

PETE: What's it like out?

STRANGER: It's raining!

PETE: That's *it!*

JOD: Go on, Pete. You're *on!* (PETE *dashes out. Curtain*)

THE END

ON YOU IT LOOKS GOOD

This skit may prove that what's sauce for the goose isn't always sauce for the gander. It takes place at a rummage sale held by the Happy Smile Club, and there is, of course, a sign that says: RUMMAGE SALE—HAPPY SMILE CLUB. *There is also another sign:* ABSOLUTELY NO EXCHANGES OR REFUNDS! *At center is a table on which all sorts of nutty garments are piled.*

❖ ❖ ❖ ❖ ❖

Characters

MRS. DEEDLE, *a lady with know-how*
ELLIE, *a young married woman*
RITA, *makes two*
MABEL, *another young married woman*
BARBARA, *a fourth innocent*

AT RISE: MRS. DEEDLE *is fluffing up the pile of garments as if it were a month's wash. She hears people coming, so she grabs her cash box and sits in a chair. She hums off-key wildly.* ELLIE, RITA, MABEL *and* BARBARA *come in, chattering to each other.*

ELLIE (*Dashing to table*): Ooooooh! All the goodies.

RITA: Wow! What lovely-looking trash.

MABEL: I *know* I'll find a bargain. I love bargains. I love bargains so much I'm always paying twice as much as they're worth.

BARBARA: I always feel at a rummage sale I'm *helping* somebody.

RITA: This one helped *me*. I got rid of four old plaid jackets of my husband's.

ELLIE: I dumped seven old brier pipes and three T-shirts with tulips on them.

BARBARA: Tulips?

ELLIE: Jim was crazy about gardening for a while.

MABEL: I gave gladly and willingly a red-white-and-blue bathrobe of Tom's.

BARBARA: Red-white-and-blue bathrobe?

MABEL: Yes. He slept overnight once at the White House. He had to have s*omething*.

ELLIE: It's for a good cause. The money is used for something or other. What *is* it used for, Mrs. Deedle?

MRS. DEEDLE: A good cause.

ELLIE: See? (*Pause*) I cleaned out Jim's closet. I was certainly glad to see that old, battered cowboy hat go. He used to wear it eating steaks outdoors. (*They are picking over stuff on the counter. ELLIE tries on a large robe. Everybody laughs. MABEL pulls on a sweater. Her sister could get in it with her.*)

MRS. DEEDLE: Sophia Loren gave that. She wore it before she lost weight.

BARBARA: Sophia Loren and who else? (*She tries on a coat that's much too tight.*)

MRS. DEEDLE: That coat was worn by Elizabeth Taylor.

BARBARA: As a child. (*They hold up various nutty garments—whatever is available: old red underwear, nightcaps, wild hats, and so on.*)

RITA: There are no prices on these things.

MRS. DEEDLE: If I put prices on them, they'd be the last and final prices. This way we can dicker.

BARBARA: That's logical. (*She picks up a hat and tries it on.*) Fits perfectly!

RITA: It's beautiful.

MRS. DEEDLE: It's *you.* (*Pause*) Five dollars.

BARBARA: Let's dicker.

MRS. DEEDLE: That's the last, final dickering price. (BARBARA *pays her.* RITA *tries on a robe that is very becoming.*)

ELLIE: Charming.

BARBARA: It's very becoming.

MRS. DEEDLE: It's *you.* Seven dollars. Final dickering price.

MABEL: It's certainly worth it. And it's for a good cause. (*While* RITA *is paying,* MABEL *tries on a coat.*)

ELLIE: Stunning.

BARBARA: Chic.

RITA: Even at a discount house, you couldn't get it for under twenty dollars.

MRS. DEEDLE: It's *you.* Twenty dollars, please. (MABEL *pays her, while* ELLIE *tries on a stole*)

RITA: Handsome.

BARBARA: A lovely stole. I had one just like it.

ELLIE: I had a coat just like the one Mabel bought.

MABEL (*To* ELLIE): That stole is a steal at any price.

MRS. DEEDLE: It's *you.* Thirty dollars. It's for a good cause. (ELLIE *pays her, while the others casually hold up stuff. Then, they start to go, wearing their purchases.* ELLIE *stops suddenly.*)

ELLIE (*To* MABEL): That's *my* coat. I just recognized it.

MABEL: Well, it's *mine* now. Someone gave it to the rummage sale.

BARBARA (*Staring at the stole*): That's my stole. Of course. No wonder I liked it.

ELLIE: I paid good money for it. Too bad.

27

RITA (*To* BARBARA): I *knew* I felt something funny about that hat. I bought it last Easter.

BARBARA: That's a pity. I just paid for it. No exchanges or refunds.

MRS. DEEDLE: It's *you.*

ALL (*To* MRS. DEEDLE): Oh, shut up! Be quiet. Is that all you can say?

MRS. DEEDLE: It's all for a good cause.

MABEL (*To* RITA): Wait a minute. (*She looks inside robe*) That's *my* robe. My husband always hated it. But it's mine.

RITA: Not any longer.

BARBARA: I think that's terrible.

MABEL: What are you complaining about?

ELLIE: Oh, don't be so innocent.

RITA: Wait! *Wait!* Let's not get all hot and bothered. Let's not break up our friendship. I can see it all now. We gave away our husbands' stuff . . . sure, it was old and wrinkled. . . .

ELLIE: Yes, but it was junk they wanted to keep.

MABEL: Sure. So they are having their revenge. They gave away all the stuff of *ours* that they didn't like.

RITA: The scoundrels!

MABEL: The cads!

ELLIE: The cheaters!

BARBARA: The tricksters. They're as bad as *we* are.

ELLIE: And we can't let them get away with *that.* Let's go home.

MRS. DEEDLE: It's all for a good cause. It's to help an underprivileged woman. Mostly *me.* (*The four women flounce out as* MRS. DEEDLE *counts her money.*)

THE END

RIDE YOUR HOBBY

The setting of this skit is The Modern Hobby Shop. A sign may say so. Another sign may say: YOUR HOBBY IS OUR HOBBY. *If possible, a long counter at center can have odds and ends: women's shoes, assorted hi-fi components or pieces of old washing machines, radios, lawn mowers that could serve as hi-fi components, etc. Also, there should be a basketball or balloon painted black and marked* 500 LBS. *and a cardboard box painted black and marked* ONE TON.

❖ ❖ ❖ ❖ ❖

Characters

PERCY LIMPID, *a psychologist and owner of a hobby shop*

GEORGE MENDEL, *who collects off-beat matchbook covers*

SAM MASTERS, *who collects slippers in case he meets Cinderella*

TIM GRIFFEN, *who collects exercises*

HARRY ASHMAN, *a hi-fi nut who likes realism*

FATS PALMER, *who eats exotic steaks*

AT RISE: PERCY LIMPID *is standing behind the junk counter.* GEORGE MENDEL, *a slim, nervous fellow, comes in.*

GEORGE: Is this the Modern Hobby Shop?

PERCY: It is. And I am Percy Limpid, owner and consulting psychologist. We like to match your hobbies to your personality.

GEORGE: I collect matchbook covers.

PERCY (*Picking up the "one ton" weight and lifting it casually up and down with one hand*): You should have an outdoor hobby. Why not shoot elephants? Keeps you out in the fresh air. Gives you exercise dodging poisoned darts. Or why not collect poisoned darts? Keeps you out in the sunny jungle with the pygmies.

GEORGE: No. Matchbook covers.

PERCY: All right. We have everything. Here. (*Indicating display*) Here are all of our matchbook covers for collectors. (*Holds one up and reads it*) "The Roman Gardens. When in Rome, don't miss Nero's Hot Fiddle. Togas starched while you eat." (*Holds up another*) Here's another from the Napoleonic era. (*Reads*) "While in St. Helena, stop at the Josephine Motor Courts. Bathtubs direct from Versailles." (*Reads from another*) How about this: "Enjoy your stay at Alcatraz. You're not leaving." (*Shows another*) Here's a dilly: "Adult Education nightly at the Academy in Athens. Every Monday hear Plato talk to himself!"

GEORGE: Gosh, are those authentic?

PERCY: Of course they're authentic. If you don't believe it, I'll draw up an old document to prove it. Signed by Plato, if you like.

GEORGE: I'll take them.

PERCY: Twelve dollars. (*Takes money* GEORGE *gives him, hands* GEORGE *covers*) Come back next week. We'll have some from the Stone Age. They read: "Come to Flathead's Cave, nightly. See a demonstration of FIRE."

GEORGE: Great! (*He goes out.* SAM MASTERS *enters.*)

SAM: I collect glass slippers. You got any?

PERCY: Certainly. But as a consulting hobby psychologist, I must say that you should be doing something intellectual. Have you ever thought of juggling?

SAM: That's intellectual?

PERCY: You juggle the *Encyclopaedia Britannica.*

SAM (*Shaking head*): Nope. I'll stick with Cinderella. I keep thinking I'll meet her. (*Dances*) Yeah, yeah, yeah.

PERCY: I have the original glass slipper from Cinderella. In fact, I have it in two sizes. (*Holds up shoes*)

SAM: How can this be explained?

PERCY: Simply. One she wore before she married the prince. Size 4½. The other she wore when she was queen. Size 10. Her feet spread, standing up saluting her subjects all day.

SAM (*Delighted*): I'll take them.

PERCY: They are thirty-two dollars plus the amusement tax. (SAM *pays, takes objects and goes.* TIM GRIFFEN *comes in. He is pale and tired.*)

TIM: I'm looking for something to exercise with . . . as a hobby.

PERCY: I agree with you. You look like someone who should have stayed in the hospital an extra six months. Now, I have some tremendous exercise equipment here. Look. (*He lifts the balloon several times.*)

TIM: Five hundred pounds?

PERCY: Lift it five hundred times a day. Then you try the one ton. (*Lifts the "one ton" weight, balances it on his head, takes it down.* TIM *goes over and feels the top of* PERCY's *head.*)

TIM: I could never lift those heavy weights.

PERCY: But that's our secret. These are the *lightest* five-hundred-pound and one-ton weights in the world. See. Try them. (TIM *picks one up and then the other, puts them under his arms.*)

TIM: A great idea. I'll take them. How much do I owe you?

PERCY: Fifty dollars. It isn't easy to make such heavy weights out of such lightweight material. It's a secret of modern science. (TIM *pays and goes out, bouncing the "500 pound" weight in one hand.* HARRY ASHMAN *enters, humming.*)

HARRY: Hi-fi is my hobby. I want to build the greatest hi-fi set ever. I want it so precise you can hear the Beatles sing.

PERCY: But the Beatles can't *sing.*

HARRY: That's how precise it has to be. I see you have a lot of components here.

PERCY: As a consulting hobby psychologist, my impression is you'd be happier skin-diving. Have you ever thought of using your skin for that purpose?

HARRY: *My* impression is you should sell me what I want. I think you're maladjusted psychosomatically, and suffering from delusions, illusions, hysteria, dandruff and isometric, barometric glandular psychoses.

PERCY: Well, if you put it in a friendly way . . . like *that* . . . we have components here you never dreamed of.

HARRY: I can see . . . like a lawn-mower blade and a washing-machine motor.

PERCY: That shows you are still an amateur.

HARRY: And some wire coat hangers . . .

PERCY: On the surface only. (*Starts twisting things together, banging them, slapping glue on them, tying rope around them, etc. Now and then* HARRY *is swept up and helps him.*) You are going to see a masterpiece of hi-fi when I get through. Notice how the weefer is amalgamated here with the toofer and the invalid is synchromeshed with the gavotte. Most hi-fi's don't even have a lap-over, throwback, and sit-down at all.

HARRY: Yeah. That would make a difference.

PERCY: See how the medulla is wrapped around the busboy for cutting out interference and fringe benefits?

HARRY: I like that pavane in there, filtering out the excessive overtones.

PERCY: Sure, but you don't notice all the little things. (*He twists wire around and slaps some glue on something, then he begins attaching anything he can find on the counter—shoes, skates, hammer, screwdriver . . . anything and everything.*) Look at the way I've eliminated all possibility of the turntable being jarred by an atom bomb. Notice that it is cushioned in Jello. Fresh Jello.

HARRY: This should really sound lifelike. If it isn't a fake.

PERCY: *Fake?* You must be a *rank* amateur. Can't you *see* the decibels plus or minus decimal five-oh-two? Look at the wind gauge that automatically keeps the record from blowing away. Notice the steam engine attached in case the electricity goes off. Notice the six speaker stereo amplifier with a cut-out and predatory post-operative pestle. (*Stands back proudly*) Now . . . we're ready. I must ask you to turn around so the sight of the components will not influence you.

HARRY: O.K. (*He turns around.*)

PERCY (*Singing, trying to sound professional*): "On the road to Mandalay. Where the flying fishes . . . uh . . . playyyy-uh. . . ." (*He sings a few bars and then stops.*) O.K.

HARRY (*Turning around, delighted*): Magnificent. I'll take it. Why, it sounded as if the singer were standing right *here*. Absolutely lifelike. How much is it?

PERCY: Two hundred dollars. I'll have to take it apart to

ship it to you, but then you want the fun of putting it together.

HARRY (*Pays*): Oh, absolutely. (*Goes out humming "On the Road to Mandalay."* FATS PALMER *comes in.*)

FATS: My hobby is exotic food. You advertise you have everything.

PERCY: Right. Kangaroo steaks. Filets of grasshopper . . . zebra chops. Fresh-frozen. Everything.

FATS: Do you have white whale?

PERCY (*A little stunned*): White whale? White whale is very scarce. Very expensive. White whale is almost non-existent.

FATS: Then you have been advertising fraudulently. No white whale.

PERCY: We said we have it and we have it. Yes. You wouldn't settle for plain whale?

FATS: White whale.

PERCY: O.K.

FATS: I want *one* steak.

PERCY: *One* white whale steak?

FATS: You have it, haven't you? Or else. . . .

PERCY (*Now calm and smiling*): We have it. Oh, we have it. But I must definitely refuse to slaughter my white whale for one, measly steak. (*Curtain*)

THE END

SWEETIE-WEETIES!

The setting of this skit is the Board Room at Plunkett's Sweetie-Weeties, Inc., and a sign might say so.

❖ ❖ ❖ ❖ ❖

Characters

MR. PLUNKETT, *president of Plunkett's Sweetie-Weeties, Inc.*

FRED ⎤ *his four brain trusters (who*
GEORGE ⎟ *can all be women, if you*
PHIL ⎟ *prefer, or any combination*
TIM ⎦ *of men and women)*

AT RISE: MR. PLUNKETT *sits at a table with his four brain trusters. The giant economy size of Sweetie-Weeties is in front of him. He takes a handful of cereal and holds it up thoughtfully.*

MR. PLUNKETT: Ah, Sweetie-Weeties! We shall now eat some Sweetie-Weeties so that we may be provided with fresh insights, new inspirations. We shall have food for thought. (*He nibbles thoughtfully. If someone offstage can make a ghastly crackling noise, it would be fun. He passes the box around. The four men sigh in turn, take a handful wearily and eat without zest. They are all making notes.* MR. PLUNKETT *blows a whistle.*) Now you have all had five minutes to work your little brains and come up with an idea for a new TV commercial for

35

Sweetie-Weeties. It has to be different. It has to be un-heard of. It has to be utterly unique in an unusual way. We have bought hundreds of one-minute spots and we have to use them in the best way possible. Fred?

FRED (*Gets up*): Well, Chief, we all know that Plunkett's Sweetie-Weeties is more than a crunchy, sugary break-fast food.

GEORGE: Right!

PHIL: It can be used to stuff sofa pillows.

TIM: Right. Mixed with a little cement and water it makes an edible stucco for plastering cellars in case you run out of food.

FRED: Right. Let's not forget it is also a tonic, containing every known vitamin, mineral and enough coffee extract to make a few good cups if you run out of coffee.

MR. PLUNKETT: Let's always keep in mind that a plaster made of hot, mushed Sweetie-Weeties can be applied to bruises and cuts since Sweetie-Weeties contains Pooh-197, a notorious antibiotic.

FRED: Exactly. Powdered and mixed with vaseline, it makes a fine hair-grooming agent.

TIM: Added to your gas tank it cleans lead deposits from your engine and stops air pollution.

PHIL: *And* when you get done with the contents, the entire *box* can be broken in pieces and spread with peanut but-ter for the children's lunches.

FRED: Correct. Now, I thought of a TV picture where we show the beginnings of America: Washington crossing the Delaware. . . . Lincoln growing his beard . . . the war with Spain . . . Old Ironsides . . . the Maine . . . San Juan Hill. (*He illustrates charging up San Juan Hill on horseback*) Yippee! Rat-tata-tat . . . bang . . . boom . . . bang, you're dead. (*He illustrates the next, too.*)

The first transcontinental train. Pooh! Pooooh! Chug-chug-chug . . . Pooh, pooh. . . . clackety-clackety-clackety . . . poooooooooh! America! Going forward . . . and everywhere a soldier or a worker with a box of Sweetie-Weeties, the economy size. Lincoln reading the Gettysburg Address and dipping into his Sweetie-Weeties . . .

MR. PLUNKETT: Too patriotic. We have huge sales in the Congo, Mexico and Nationalist China, for example.

TIM (*Gets up*): I felt, Chief, that something simple and delicate and romantic . . . well . . . there's this boy and girl sharing a box of Sweetie-Weeties. They gaze at each other. (*He shows how.*) They crunch their flakes and gaze again. He takes her hand. They begin to dance on a fake cloud. They sing. (*He sings.*)

> Sweetie-Weetie sugar pie,
> I'm for you, you're for I.
> Sweetie-Weetie lovey dove
> Is the food for falling in love.
> Tra la la . . . la la. . . .

(*He dances around, first as the girl, then as the boy.*)

MR. PLUNKETT: No, no. Too corny. How about you, Phil?

PHIL: I'd like something that doesn't directly concern the product. For example, we have the Boston Symphony Orchestra play a one-minute classical piece with Horowitz at the piano. The only sign of the product is that Horowitz—who is very agile—dips into a box of Sweetie-Weeties when he has a few moments where he uses only his left hand. See? We could commission all the great composers to write the Sweetie-Weetie Concerto.

MR. PLUNKETT: People don't like classical music. You notice the "Emperor Concerto" has *never* made the Top Twenty. *Not once* in all the years it's had. No! George?

37

GEORGE (*Gets up*): I had in mind a film showing the many uses of Sweetie-Weeties. (*He illustrates.*) A woman walks along the street and she feels faint. (*He illustrates.*) She reels. She staggers. She leans against a post and starts eating from a box of Sweetie-Weeties. In a moment she is smiling, walking along briskly and singing "My country, 'tis of thee." Another fellow has been bruised. He howls with pain. (*Howls, jumps up and down*) Ouch! Ouch! I caught my nose in the meat grinder! Suddenly someone slaps a poultice of Sweetie-Weeties on his nose. He smiles and sighs with relief, licking what slips down into his mouth. A car is stalled. Chugga—agrrooooo . . . oink . . . agaroo . . . screech. The man gets out, throws some Sweetie-Weeties under the tire and zoom . . . brrrrrrrr . . . off goes the car! A woman . . .

MR. PLUNKETT: No. No, no, no. Too crass. Too obvious. We've been advertising *all* this stuff everywhere for twenty years. Everybody *knows* what Sweetie-Weeties are and what they do. Everybody. (*Pause*) Think, everyone! We have to come up with something.

TIM: I think I have it, boss. People have been watching television for hours. (*Illustrates*) Bang-bang. Wheeeeeee. Murders. Police cars. Calling Dr. Soggy. Calling Nurse Nervous Nellie! Hillbillies twanging away . . . yah—yah—yaaah . . . be my honey bee, I'll be your pet-oon-a—eee . . . Comedians telling jokes . . . "Is your wife entertaining this winter?" "Not very." "How's your wife?" "Compared to what?" All this junk, endlessly, day after day . . . so what do *we* do?

MR. PLUNKETT (*Interested*): What *do* we do?

TIM: We say, "Plunkett's Sweetie-Weeties bring you one solid minute of *nothing*. N O T H I N G. Nothing."

And we have a minute of plain, everyday, soothing *Nothing*.

MR. PLUNKETT: Great! Magnificent. Why didn't I think of that?

FRED: Marvelous!

GEORGE: A great prestige builder!

PHIL: A boon to eyes and ears.

ALL: Nothing! Nothing!

MR. PLUNKETT: A wonderful, beautiful television screen full of *nothing!* (*All shake hands with each other happily, repeating, "Nothing!" as the curtain falls.*)

THE END

IT'S FRIGHTENING!

This skit takes place in the boss's office of Infamous Tele-vision Productions, Inc. A sign says: WE BELIEVE IN GOOD TASTE AS LONG AS IT PAYS. *Still another sign says:* IF IT SELLS SOAP, IT'S GOOD. *At center is a desk, which should be placed at an angle. A chair is behind the desk, and several chairs face the desk. Anything by way of decoration would be good—anything that suggests TV, drama, people, and sales charts.*

❖ ❖ ❖ ❖ ❖

Characters

CHAUNCEY ZIPPO, *the boss of Infamous*
 Television Productions, Inc.

TOM
DICK   *workers in the world of*
HARRY   *television, creators of junk*
CHARLEY

MONSTER, *a monster*

AT RISE: TOM, DICK, HARRY *and* CHARLEY *are seated in chairs, facing the desk. They ad lib conversation to each other for a moment until* CHAUNCEY ZIPPO *enters. As* CHAUNCEY *walks to his chair behind the desk, the others stand and bow their heads.* CHAUNCEY *sits, picks up a Chinese gong (or something of the sort) from his desk, and sounds the gong. The others sit.*

CHAUNCEY: I suppose you wonder why I made you leave your comfy homes to come down here to Infamous Television Productions, Incorporated.

TOM: Well, sir. . . .

CHAUNCEY (*Glares and strikes gong*): *I'll* tell you when to speak. The fact is, I couldn't sleep. We *have* to come up with something new and fresh and half-witted for the coming television season. Something original for the boob-tube. Something unusual for the idiot box. Something. . . .

DICK: I was thinking, O Wise One, that. . . .

CHAUNCEY (*Strikes gong*): I'll tell you when to start thinking. (*Strikes gong again*) Now, when I ask for ideas, I don't want old cut-and-dried, last week's bread-pudding stuff. I want something 100% tried-and-true—and unheard of. I want something sure-fire in an experimental vein. I want something that combines the Beatles and a murder trial with a Presidential press conference and an orgy of poetry recitations by Elizabeth Taylor in a bathing suit. I want something *big* . . . something subtle . . . something clever, witty, and brilliant that any moron can understand. What's your idea, Tom?

TOM: How about hillbillies? Mountain folk are funny. They're dirty, ignorant and penniless. People find this very amusing. They sing a lot, too. (*Sings*) "Oooooh, iffen I had someone to cook my turnips . . . oooooh . . ."

CHAUNCEY (*Strikes gong sharply*): Hillbillies are old stuff. Beverly Hillbillies . . . New York Hillbillies . . . London Hillbillies. . . . Walter O'Keefe had hillbillies on radio for ten years . . . Snuffy Smith has them in the comic strips . . . hillbillies . . . in a word . . . are definitely *out*. Dick?

DICK: I was thinking about doctors and nurses I

41

mean *real* doctors and nurses. Every week we could go to a real hospital and follow a doctor around. . . .

CHAUNCEY: Doctors and nurses are old-hat. Even real ones. Real ones would be worse. Dr. Kildare . . . Nurse Kookie . . . doll surgeons . . . dog surgeons . . . they give me a pain. Well, Harry?

HARRY: While you were all talking, I was thinking . . . how about private detectives?

CHAUNCEY (*Strikes gong hard*): Private detectives? Phooey! District Attorneys? Double phooey with cream cheese. Policemen, triple phooey!

HARRY: I meant something new in detectives. For example, what about a private detective who can fly? Really fly! He has wings he hides under his winter underwear.

CHAUNCEY (*Strikes the gong*): Harry, believe me, you're a hard worker and a good team man . . . but don't *push* it. Charley?

CHARLEY: I've been making a study of the phenomena of viewing TV and the subconscious demands of tele-viewers.

CHAUNCEY: O.K. Never mind that. You don't impress me. I flunked out of the same high school you did. With honors.

CHARLEY: There are only a few things left for the viewer to respond to. Puppets . . . talking dolphins . . . leprechauns . . . and monsters.

CHAUNCEY: *Monsters!* (*He strikes the gong wildly*) Monsters! I knew I'd think of it. It was just a matter of someone nudging me. Next season it's monsters! Everybody loves monsters. Something that eats people and throws people up against walls and turns them into fish . . . and knocks down all the buildings in town! Real excitement! Suspense! All my life I've been fond of monsters.

You can't blame *them* for what they do. That's how they're *made.*

TOM: But what kind of monster will we have, sir?

CHAUNCEY: Just what I was going to ask. We have Frankensteins . . . we have Mr. Hydes . . . we have Things from the Slimy Lagoon . . . we have Teen-age Werewolves . . . we have Mechanical Men with their brains gone astray. Tom, go to the make-up room and come back with some new kind of monster. (TOM *dashes out.*) Monsters!

DICK (*Enthusiastically*): Yes, monsters! They reflect the domination of the ego-centered drive.

HARRY: To say nothing of the repressed recognitions.

CHARLEY: We'll be benefactors. We'll straighten out any warped personalities in the audience. (TOM *comes back as Frankenstein or some other monster. He wears a mask.*)

TOM: How's this?

CHAUNCEY (*Strikes gong*): No. It doesn't scare me. You try, Dick. (DICK *runs out as* TOM *removes his mask and sits.*)

TOM: This monster idea will be sensational.

HARRY: We can have puppets who are monsters . . . fish who are monsters.

CHARLEY: We can turn everyone and everything into monsters. (DICK *comes back with coat on backwards and a head coming out of his shoulder or something like that.*)

DICK: I eat people and repel mosquitoes. Grrrr!

CHAUNCEY (*Strikes his chest*): It doesn't get me—*here.* Harry, you try. You have to think of something really frightening and scary that will make viewers a little sick —but not sick enough to turn off the set. (HARRY *goes off, while* DICK *sits down.*)

43

TOM: We'll make all those viewers just a *little* sick. (*He holds his head.*)

DICK (*Holding stomach*): Not *too* sick.

CHARLEY: Just sick enough to be glued to their chairs. (HARRY *comes in. He is wearing a green suit and flippers, and the head of an alligator or something equally disturbing. Ingenuity can be used here. An extra eye might be painted in the middle of the head, an extra arm might be added—things like that.*)

HARRY: I almost scared myself when I saw me in the mirror. Of course, I should have horns and an extra set of teeth, maybe—also a tail with a saw on it.

CHAUNCEY (*Hits gong*): No! Cheap stuff. It doesn't *do* anything. This monster has to frighten people out of their wits so that they need to come back for more. O.K., Charley. Someone has to do this right. (CHARLEY *goes out as* HARRY *sits down.*)

TOM: Don't worry, boss. Good old Charley. He'll come up with something.

DICK: Charley has talent. He can do anything.

HARRY: Charley will create the monster to out-monster monsters. (*All of them look eagerly to door. The most horrible* MONSTER *conceivable appears. It is much taller than a man—maybe one man on another's shoulders, or a dog on a man's shoulders with a tail wagging out from under his hat. The whole* MONSTER *might be covered with a skeleton costume, with cats' heads sticking out of the pockets and some kind of head leering out from behind . . . anything wild and wonderful and frightening. The* MONSTER *walks in laboriously, perhaps with a chicken in his claw or a stuffed owl on a stick like a lollipop.*)

CHAUNCEY (*Delighted*): Miraculous. So real! So lifelike.

Charley, this is your night of triumph. Charley, you have done it! If I didn't know you were in that costume, Charley, I'd be scared to death. (MONSTER *comes closer to* CHAUNCEY *who keeps shaking his head and smiling.*) We'll call you the Nightmare Lizard . . . or . . . Dracula's Bad Dream. Charley, you are wonderful! (*At this point,* CHARLEY *comes in. He doesn't notice* MONSTER *immediately. He speaks to* CHAUNCEY)

CHARLEY: Boss, something happened in the make-up room. The make-up man disappeared. Nothing but his shoes left.

CHAUNCEY (*To* MONSTER): Charley, you can be sure we'll use this. (*Looks at real* CHARLEY) Charley . . . I . . . you . . . *Charley!*

CHARLEY: Boss . . . I . . . you . . . (*He stares at the* MONSTER, *then at the others. All of them suddenly realize what has happened. They rush out, frightened. The* MONSTER *watches them go, roars, then picks up a chair and tries to eat it as the curtains close.*)

THE END

THE CAMPING PICTURES

The scene is the living room of Brenda's home. There is a projector set up facing the audience. It is evening.

❖ ❖ ❖ ❖ ❖

Characters
BRENDA, *who has been on a camping trip into the wilderness and is showing slides of it*
KATHY *friends of* BRENDA'S, *who*
BEA *come to cheer and leave*
NANCY *baffled*

AT RISE: BEA *and* KATHY *are sitting in straight chairs near the projector.* BEA *looks at her watch.*

BEA: I just can't *wait* to see Brenda's slides. Imagine! Two girls going on a rough camping trip with just a tent, a sleeping bag and an old car!

KATHY: I wouldn't *dare* go camping. I'd be afraid of noises in the night.

BEA: Like what?

KATHY: Like tigers or muskrats or fleas . . . anything.

BEA: I guess I just wasn't born to rough it, either. But I certainly admire Brenda and Lulu.

KATHY: Brenda said most of the time they cooked out, too. You know—cans of beans over a campfire. And when they caught a fish they fried it.

NANCY (*Coming in*): Isn't this exciting? I think Brenda and

Lulu are wonderful. Not many pretty young girls would give up a glamorous two weeks and spend the time hiking, climbing mountains, sleeping in a tent or under the stars in a sleeping bag.

KATHY: Doing washing with a stone in a trout stream.

BEA: Didn't they get trout all over their clothes?

NANCY: No. The trout keep to their own side. (*Pause*) Taking a bath in a tiny brook, scenting themselves with pine needles.

KATHY: Oh, here comes Brenda now with the slides. (*Pause*) Hi! (BRENDA *comes in with a box of slides. She walks proudly and smiles in a self-satisfied way.*)

BRENDA: I'm so glad you all could come. I think we can start right away. (*She puts in a slide and then laughs awkwardly.*) Upside down. (*Straightens it*) There! (*Stares*) Oh, that's the Christmas tree last year. It got mixed in. (*Puts another slide in*) There we are! Starting off in the old, broken-down '56 Chevy.

KATHY (*Peering and squinting*): Looks more like a '66 Caddy.

BRENDA (*Changing picture*): Well, we wanted the old broken-down Chevy but my father thought we'd be safer in the Caddy. Here we are packing the tent and the sleeping bag.

BEA: Who's that with you?

BRENDA: Oh, that's Papa's chauffeur. He helped us pack. (*Another slide*) This is our first stop in the Adirondacks. Utter wilderness except for the hooting of owls and the screams of wildcats.

KATHY: Everything looks awfully red.

BRENDA: Yes, we kindled a fire, Indian fashion, and it spread quite a way . . . American fashion. (*Another slide*) Here we are, getting breakfast at dawn after the fire had been put out.

NANCY: Isn't that the Lake Placid Woodsy Restaurant?

BRENDA: Yes. The people camping around us took up a collection so we could eat in town. Old scaredy-cat campers, thought we might be careless with our fire. Hmph! . (*Another slide*) Here we are starting to climb Old Rugged Goatface Mountain, highest in the Adirondacks.

KATHY: In sneakers and kilts?

BRENDA: We thought of that right after the picture was taken. (*Another slide*) Here, you see us in full regalia, completely equipped.

NANCY: High heels? Evening gowns?

BRENDA (*Impatiently*): We decided to go dancing that night and start climbing the next morning. (*Another slide*) Here is Lulu's date.

BEA: He certainly needs a shave.

NANCY: A beatnik!

BRENDA: Sorry. That's a grizzly bear who posed for us the next day.

KATHY: I thought he had awfully big feet!

BRENDA: Oh, dear, these slides seem to be a bit mixed up. This . . . uh . . . (*Narrows eyes*) Well, it was supposed to be *my* date but it looks like the Leaning Tower of Pisa. (*She squints at another slide, puzzled.*) This is a picture of me starting to put up the tent but I have roses growing out of my head and a train creeping up my back.

NANCY: It must be a double exposure.

BRENDA (*New slide*): Here's the tent after we got it up the first night.

KATHY: It has horses in it.

BRENDA: Yes. The horses loved it. Kept off the flies. *We* had to get out. (*New slide*) Here it is, later.

BEA: I don't see anything but woods.

BRENDA: The tent blew down into a ravine. We had to sleep under the stars in our sleeping bags. (*New slide*)

This is Lulu in her sleeping bag at the foot of Old Goat-face . . . (*Squints, puzzled*) I guess this slide got mixed in. Lulu's giving me my Christmas present under our tree. It was a cute golden charm bracelet. (*New slide*) Ah, there's Lulu in her sleeping bag. She couldn't get the zipper shut.

NANCY: What are those two big animals at the front?

BRENDA: Those are Lulu's feet. The bag was too short. (*New slide*) This is a cow.

KATHY: It *is?*

BRENDA: Isn't it? It came right up to us and was very friendly.

BEA: *That* is a wolf . . . a snarling wolf.

BRENDA (*Nervously*): I thought it was an awfully *small* cow. (*Laughs shakily*) Ha, ha! No wonder it ate our fried chicken.

KATHY: Fried chicken? I thought you were going to trap or fish for your own food.

BRENDA: Well, the first night we decided it would be silly to shoot chicken. (*New slide*) Anyway . . . the next morning we explored into wilderness where no college freshman had ever been. I don't *think* any had been there . . . there were no signs of lipsticks or stuff. See? Indian country. These are the . . . Goatface Indians, I believe. This group—the Chief, his squaw, several braves and a couple of cowards—had never seen white girls before. That's what they said.

KATHY: What's that in back . . . out there in the savage country?

BRENDA: That's a wigwam.

BEA: It looks like a station wagon.

BRENDA: I know. It's a Chrysler Wigwam. (*New slide*) Here, the Chief and I . . .

NANCY: What was his name?

BRENDA: Huh? Oh. Well, his Goatface name was Fast Running Deer Over the Trout Brook. He told us to call him Bob. Here we are doing a secret tribal dance no white woman had ever before danced. It was called the Bangles, Beads and Feathers Cha-Cha. (*New slide*) Here we are, at last, ready to climb Goatface.

BEA: In bathing suits?

BRENDA: It was terribly hot and we had decided to go swimming instead. (*New slide*) This is the primitive Indian chief again . . . at the sixth hole of the Wilderness Golf Club. Here we are, at last, on top of Old Goatface. We . . . there had been a bit of a landslide . . . nothing serious. This is really Old Goatface on top of *us*. (*New slide*) Ah, here we are . . . exhausted, weary, hungry, thirsty and out-of-breath . . . but, *finally*. . . .

NANCY: What's that behind you?

BRENDA (*Laughs uneasily*): That's the hotel's helicopter. It flies you up to Old Goatface Hotel. The Old Goatface Hilton. We thought it would be more exciting than climbing. (*Pause*) Ahem. Here is the last slide as we get ready for bed in the hotel. The hot water was cool, they had stopped serving dinner, and you could get only one station on the color TV. Of course we didn't mind. Ha, ha. We had deliberately set out to rough it. And we hadn't brought a nickel with us. Just a credit card. (*New slide*) We refused to sleep in the soft feather beds. Here we are on the floor in our sleeping bags . . . eating some lobster stuffed with shrimp that the chef managed to throw together for us. You can't beat the simple life. We didn't even have napkins! (*Curtain*)

THE END

OH, MEDICO!

This is a skit about doctors. Not the real ones who get up at two in the morning and bring you cough syrup, but the TV and radio and movie doctors. They take care of everything from heartbreak to heartburn.

The setting of this study is the West Wing of the North Hospital. The three doctors who appear don't have doctors' suits on. Anyone can look like a doctor by putting his shirt on backwards and carrying a large corkscrew in his pocket. Or a large knife.

It would be nice to have a sign that says: HOSPITAL: NO ROCK 'N' ROLL. *By the sign (which is in a hallway) is a table or stretcher. On the table is the "patient"—all covered up by a sheet, except for a small portion that could be a head. It could also be a squash.*

❖ ❖ ❖ ❖ ❖

Characters
DR. KILMARE, *a doctor*
DR. CASEY, *also a doctor*
DR. LIVINGSTONE, *a strolling doctor*

AT RISE: *The "patient" is on the table. After a moment,* DR. KILMARE *comes in. He stares at the "patient." He takes a knife out and sharpens a pencil.* DR. CASEY *comes in, sees* DR. KILMARE *by table, and pushes him aside.*

DR. CASEY: This is *my* patient, Dr. Kilmare. Don't ham it up around *me*. Have you no ethics?

DR. KILMARE: Ethics? I have some in a red-and-white capsule, take three times a day before breakfast. Discontinue if your head shrinks.

DR. CASEY: I won't bicker with you, Kilmare, you show-off. I am a doctor because I wish to ease the pain and suffering of the human race. I have always been this way. When I was a small boy and people asked me what I wanted to be I said, "Florence Nightingale."

DR. KILMARE: Professional pride prevents me from saying that all the patients south of room 228 are mine. That's how we staked out this hospital.

DR. CASEY: Because of crowded conditions due to my popularity, this patient has had to stay in the hallway. My contract calls for all patients in the hallway.

DR. KILMARE: Not so, Casey. My contract gives me residuals and overflows.

DR. CASEY: I saw him first.

DR. KILMARE: You haven't seen him at all yet. Where's his record?

DR. CASEY (*Takes out a card*): I have it here. (*Reads*) "Patient 127, somewhere in the hall. Assigned to Dr. Casey . . . uh . . . suffering from extenuating circumstances and severe cacophony of the left tweeter . . . and complications."

DR. KILMARE: Casey, you're making that up. You're cheating. Just as you cheated in the softball game against the nurses.

DR. CASEY: I didn't cheat. Home plate was my rubber cushion and second base was my water bottle. I just decided to take them home in the fifth inning.

DR. KILMARE: We weren't playing for *keeps*.

DR. CASEY (*Ignores him, steps toward "patient"*): Odd bulges under my patient's sheet. His head seems to be where his feet should be.

DR. KILMARE: He may be lying on his stomach.

DR. CASEY: It's not only that. It's the proportions. His head is twice as big as a head. His feet appear to be like small carrots.

DR. KILMARE: A possible case of Beef Stew Disease. The toes turn to carrots and the head to a cabbage.

DR. CASEY: Where did you go to medical school?

DR. KILMARE: I went to acting school. Who needs medical school?

DR. CASEY: Kilmare, I insist you do not touch my patient. He already seems to be twisted up in a curious position.

DR. KILMARE: Possibly a wrestler who couldn't get out of a toe hold. We may be dealing with two patients here. They can't get them apart.

DR. CASEY: I'll decide that, Kilmare.

DR. KILMARE: Listen, Casey, you want to help the sick. Do me a favor. Stick to horses.

DR. CASEY: Kilmare, we signed an agreement when we came into the hospital. We staked out territories. We divided up movie, radio and TV rights.

DR. KILMARE: I never did find out who has the musical comedy rights to me.

DR. CASEY: That's not the point. Under the terms of our agreement, this patient is mine.

DR. KILMARE: I don't know why you're so stubborn.

DR. CASEY: I have to do a television show in an hour.

DR. KILMARE: Your patient may be the head nurse's Great Dane.

DR. CASEY: If he has Blue Shield, I'll take him. He won't complain about the food. He'll eat an intern.

DR. KILMARE: I'm afraid I'll have to take this patient, Casey. The TV cameras will be on me in *ten* minutes.

DR. CASEY: I'm afraid I must ask you to step aside. I have territorial rights here. (DR. LIVINGSTONE, *an elderly, slow-moving doctor, who is a little near-sighted, comes toward* CASEY *and* KILMARE. *In fact, he bumps right into them.*)

DR. LIVINGSTONE: I beg your pardon. Are you chaps the elevator?

DR. CASEY: The elevator is across the hall.

DR. LIVINGSTONE: Oh, I see. Or, rather, I don't . . . not very well without my glasses. I have to perform an operation in a half-hour, and I haven't had my lunch yet.

DR. CASEY: Very hard to operate on an empty stomach.

DR. LIVINGSTONE: It depends on the diagnosis. (*Pause*) You two are . . . ?

DR. CASEY: I'm the famous Dr. Casey.

DR. KILMARE: I'm the even more famous Dr. Kilmare.

DR. LIVINGSTONE: I'm Dr. Livingstone, chief surgeon, chief doctor, chief treasurer, chairman of the board and quite healthy at 85 except for a touch of emeritus . . . and a loss of eyesight. Did a gall bladder operation the other day. Missed completely. Removed a football from the locker. No harm done. (*Pause*) But you chaps aren't real doctors. You're actors. You have no licenses.

DR. CASEY: The patients trust us. And it gives us experience.

DR. KILMARE: When we begin and the patient knows who we are, he's full of hope.

DR. LIVINGSTONE: What is he a week later?

DR. CASEY: He generally isn't around a week later.

DR. LIVINGSTONE: I'll have to look into this. They said my lunch would be by the elevator. (*Moves and bumps into*

54

"patient"). Ah! This must be it. (*Turns to* CASEY *and* KILMARE) I'll have to check into you fellows.

DR. CASEY: Lunch?

DR. KILMARE: Lunch?

DR. LIVINGSTONE: Yes, lunch. The attendants heard the lunch bell ring, and dropped everything here. They're getting very independent. (*He pulls the cloth off the "patient," and holds up the various items he takes from the table.*) Ah, yes. Roast chicken . . . a whole one. Fresh carrots. A nice cabbage. Layer cake . . . a whole one. And my old comfortable shoes, up here. I wore my tight ones this morning. (*Starts humming*) I'm failing in many ways, but I have never lost my appetite. Nor my memory. See you later, Dr. Hammersmith and Dr. Cutlet. (*He goes out.*)

DR. CASEY: Well, Kilmare, I never thought I'd see the day when you wanted a roast chicken for a patient.

DR. KILMARE: Casey, always remember, Florence Nightingale would have been proud of us.

THE END

TO THE MOON

The scene is the launching pad where Happy Johnson is about to be launched on a space flight that will make him the first man on the moon. The space craft is standing by. It could be any old thing made of five-gallon milk cans, old wheels, tin sheeting, aluminum foil, discarded tricycles, old boilers, etc.

❖ ❖ ❖ ❖ ❖

Characters

HAPPY JOHNSON
ELLIE, *his girl friend*
FATHER
MOTHER
GENERAL PLUNK, *from the Space Agency*
AGENT, *from the Universal Life Insurance Company*

AT RISE: HAPPY, ELLIE, MOTHER, FATHER, *and* GENERAL PLUNK *are standing around the space craft.* HAPPY *is very nervous in his space suit. (It can be a space suit or a frogman's suit or a Halloween costume as long as it is wild and exotic.) The* AGENT *hurries on, waving some papers at* HAPPY. HAPPY *backs away from him.*

HAPPY: No, no! I tell you for the tenth time, I *have* enough life insurance.

AGENT: But I represent the Universal Life Insurance Company. We have branches everywhere. Our policy guarantees you a steady income after your demise.

HAPPY: Look, you've been following me everywhere for days, trying to sell me that policy. Now get lost.

AGENT: Think of your loved ones gathered here. Suppose you lose your way to the moon? Suppose you have a rear-end collision.

HAPPY: Nonsense! (*Goes to craft, pats it. It shakes and almost falls apart.*)

GENERAL: Everything is A-Okay, hunky-dory, rooty-tooty for the first manned flight to the moon. You have about a minute before this thing falls apart . . . er . . . that is . . . starts on its historic flight. Nervous?

HAPPY: Who . . . m-m-me? (*He shakes and leans against ship. It rattles. He jumps back.*) You sure this ship can stand the rigors of a flight to the moon and back?

GENERAL: And *back?* (*Takes out papers and goes through them, puzzled*)

FATHER (*To* HAPPY): I don't hold with these new contraptions. Got my watch caught in your mother's garbage disposal this morning.

MOTHER (*To* HAPPY): I want you to be very careful. Did you bring an umbrella and rubbers? Here. I packed a lunch for you. Your favorite sandwiches. Cold beans and raspberry jelly.

HAPPY: Gee, thanks, Mom. You're a real mom, Mom.

FATHER: Do you have plenty of blankets? It's cold on the moon. I don't know what you want to go to the moon for. You haven't even been to Atlantic City.

ELLIE (*To* HAPPY): Do be careful, Happy. You know I love you.

HAPPY: I love you, too. Soon as I get back we'll be married. If you'll have me.

AGENT: *If* he gets back. And I certainly hope he does. Love is a beautiful thing and marriage is a lovely experience. But if you *don't* get back . . . I suggest this accident, fire, tornado, life, loss of hair and teeth policy. It's only $9.67 a week for forty-seven years and then we start paying. Now. . . .

HAPPY: I told you I'm *not* interested. (AGENT *shrugs and goes off.*)

FATHER: That space ship got a brake on it?

HAPPY: Oh, sure. Push-button gear shifts, power steering, television, movies, running water, tile bathroom . . . everything.

MOTHER: Oh, I hope nothing happens to you.

HAPPY (*Nervously*): Don't *say* that. What could happen? (*He taps the ship and it nearly collapses.* GENERAL *holds it together.*)

GENERAL: We need a few rolls of adhesive tape and some hairpins.

MOTHER (*To* HAPPY): Suppose you get lost?

ELLIE: He got lost coming back from Forest Park last night. Ended up in East Longmeadow.

HAPPY: You can't get lost in a space ship. It's controlled automatically.

FATHER: Your mother's garbage disposal is controlled automatically but I caught my watch in it.

HAPPY: Everything is A-Okay, hotsy-totsy, hoop-dee-doo, hunky-dory, yeah . . . yeah . . . yeah.

ELLIE: I'm so glad you're confident.

HAPPY: Eight hundred million dollars have been spent on this project, and four years of work on me. I'm keen. I'm razor-edge sharp. I'm in the pink of condition. I'm a perfect American specimen. (*Pause*) I could use an aspirin, though. (*Holds his head*) It's just the excitement. I've never been to the moon before.

MOTHER: Did you bring your long underwear? And your toy trains?

FATHER: I wish you luck, son, but I still think you'd have been better off going into the dehydrated soup business with me.

MOTHER: His name will go down in history!

FATHER: So did Cleopatra's, but a lot of good it did her.

GENERAL: I think we're ready, Captain. (*Pause*) As ready as we'll ever be. (*To others*) You always have to work the bugs out of these things.

MOTHER: I hate bugs. Can't you spray?

FATHER: He means little things that go wrong . . . like the machine going sideways instead of up.

GENERAL: Or exploding. Little things like that.

ELLIE: Exploding?

HAPPY (*Very nervously, knees buckling*): Don't worry. I have a parachute. (*Pause*) Also, if the main capsule explodes, there's an inner capsule that won't do anything but get hot.

GENERAL: That's right. Well, in we go.

HAPPY (*Shaking*): In we go. Ha-ha-ha. See you soon. I'll drop you a postcard. Don't call me. I'll call you. Ha-ha-ha. (*He gets in space ship. It falls apart.* GENERAL *and others push it together.* HAPPY *sticks head out and waves. A wheel or something falls off.*)

MOTHER: Don't play cards with any strangers!

GENERAL: Ready for the countdown. (*He takes out a transistor radio and speaks into it.*) General Plunk here. Eh? What say? No. I do *not* want the . . . what? Oh, my wife. Put her on. (*Listens*) Uh-huh. Uh-huh. Well, I'm

59

sending a craft to the moon right now. As soon as I can. Yes, I'll stop at the market and get some kidneys and some grass seed. I don't think the two will taste right together, but whatever you say. Hello . . . main depot. Control tower? Ready for moon shot, manned? Ready for culmination of Project Wasted Millions? Let's go, men. Nine, eight, seven, six, four . . .

MOTHER: You left out five.

GENERAL: Right. I'm nervous.

FATHER: *You're* nervous!

GENERAL: Five, three, two, one! Off we go, into the wild blue yonder, tra-la-la . . . eight hundred million shot . . . hoop-dee-dooo into the wild blue . . . (*Shouting*) Happy! Take it out of neutral. I think your parking brake is on. (*They all wait tensely. There is a roaring sound and a great flash.*) There he goes! (*Pause*) I *think*.

CURTAIN
* * * *

If possible, the scene should now be changed slightly. There might be a lunar landscape . . . or white sheets hanging around to suggest icebergs . . . or big salad bowls to suggest dimples in the moon's crust. There should be a large sign: WELCOME TO THE MOON. BIGGEST LITTLE SATELLITE AROUND.

The space ship is still there. HAPPY *comes out of it, looks around, and then looks down as if he is looking at the Earth.*

HAPPY (*To himself*): I must remember not to breathe too much. No air here. I have to mail these postcards, too. (*Pause*) So this is the moon! Looks like Bridgeport at midnight.

AGENT (*Hurries on, waving papers at* HAPPY): How do you do. I represent the Universal Life Insurance Company. Branches everywhere. Now, our Life, Accident and Glacier Insurance protects you against windburn, glare, frostbite. . . . (*He chases the protesting* HAPPY *around the space craft as the curtain falls quickly.*)

THE END

THE PERSONALITY PROBLEM

This is a tale of tortured and twisted personalities. It takes place in a doctor's office on Park Avenue, at about three o'clock in the afternoon, when a Park Avenue doctor gets around to taking his one o'clock appointments.

❖ ❖ ❖ ❖ ❖

Characters
DR. SMOGEN, *a personality adjuster*
SMYRNA, *his wife, who needs him*
MR. GIMP, *a nice enough fellow who thinks he's a dog*
MRS. GIMP, *his attractive wife who is fairly certain he isn't*

AT RISE: DR. SMOGEN *is dusting a sign that says:* COME TO DR. SMOGEN WITH YOUR PERSONALITY PROBLEMS. *He moves over to a sign reading:* KEEP YOUR TEMPER! *This is a bit crooked, and while he adjusts it, it falls down and he jumps up and down angrily, stamping his feet and banging his fist. After a few moments he looks up at a sign that says:* SMILE. *So he smiles. What else?*

At this point his wife, SMYRNA, *comes in. The smile leaves the* DOCTOR'S *face as* SMYRNA *gaily hops about the room, chicken-fashion, waving her arms like wings and saying, "Chick-chick-chick" and other definitely chicken noises. She clucks and clicks and pecks her head at the desk. The* DOCTOR *finally takes up a box from behind the desk, labelled* CHICKEN FEED *and puts some corn in* SMYRNA'S *hand. She gobbles a little.*

DOCTOR: Smyrna, my dearest wife, with your personality problem I wish you wouldn't come around the office. You give it a bad name.

SMYRNA (*Nods, smiles, nibbles corn, flutters her wings, hopping toward the exit*): Cluck-cluck-cluck . . . cluck-cluck.

DOCTOR (*Matter-of-factly*): Cock-a-doodle-do. And many of them. (SMYRNA *goes out.* DOCTOR *sits down with his head in his hands. In a moment* MR. *and* MRS. GIMP *enter. She is an attractive woman, worried at the moment. He is a pleasant enough man, but he is now down on his hands and knees, smiling, wiggling in friendly fashion, and barking.*)

DOCTOR (*Looks up*): Something the matter, Mrs. Gimp?

MRS. GIMP: Well . . . it all depends . . . I. . . .

DOCTOR: I think your dog is overdressed.

MRS. GIMP: Possibly, but . . .

DOCTOR: Part beagle, isn't he?

MRS. GIMP: I'm not sure, but . . .

DOCTOR (*Puts on glasses*): Strangely human-looking. Isn't that odd?

MRS. GIMP: Not when you consider he's my husband, Dr. Smogen. (MR. GIMP *smiles, wags and barks.*)

DOCTOR: Really? He's acting normal for a dog, but not very normal for a husband. Ha-ha.

MRS. GIMP: I know you can help him. He certainly has a personality problem.

DOCTOR: I agree. I notice he shaved this morning. For a

dog that would be unusual. For a husband, it's common-place. It would appear he can't make up his mind which to be. Does he chase other dogs?

MRS. GIMP: No. He just chases trucks.

DOCTOR: Have you any idea how this transformation started?

MRS. GIMP: Well, I've often *told* him he was in the dog-house . . . and one day about a month ago I left his dinner on the stove—I thought it was corned beef hash, but it was dog food. He never noticed. Said he loved it. That night he slept under the bed.

DOCTOR (*As* MR. GIMP *crawls over to him and acts friendly*): Very friendly dog . . . er . . . husband . . . or whatever.

MRS. GIMP: You *can* help him, can't you?

DOCTOR: If he *wants* to be helped.

MRS. GIMP: He still talks a little.

DOCTOR: Good. (*To* MR. GIMP.) How much is three and three?

MR. GIMP: Five.

DOCTOR: How much is four and four?

MR. GIMP: Five.

DOCTOR: How much is seven and two?

MR. GIMP: Five.

DOCTOR: Consistent, anyway. I like that in a man . . . *or* a dog.

MRS. GIMP: He's very smart. (*To* MR. GIMP) Stand up and *beg*. (MR. GIMP *stands up and begs.*) Fetch! Fetch! (MR. GIMP *gets down on all fours, crawls to table and brings back newspaper.*) Sing! (MR. GIMP *throws back his head and lets out a canine yowl that yet has a certain melodious quality*)

DOCTOR: Ah, yes . . . an aria from *La Traviata*. (*To* MR.

GIMP) Now, Mr. Gimp, you are *not* a dog. You are deluding yourself. You are escaping from your problems by assuming the spirit of a dog. (MR. GIMP *just wags and scampers and sits up, dog-like.*) You are not a dog. (*To* MRS. GIMP) Sometimes a little hypnotism works! You are not a dog. You are not a dog. You are *not* a dog. (*Waves his fingers in* MR. GIMP's *face*)

MRS. GIMP: I hope he's convinced now. We went out to dinner last night and he saw a sign, NO DOGS ALLOWED. He wouldn't go in.

DOCTOR: Perhaps we can approach him on his own level. (*He gets down on all fours*) Arrfff! Arrrrf! Hello, fellow doggie! (MR. GIMP *looks at* DOCTOR *a little suspiciously.*)

MRS. GIMP: He doesn't trust you.

DOCTOR: You get down, too. (MRS. GIMP *gets down on all fours.* MR. GIMP *arrffs playfully, wags gaily and moves around as if expecting to be chased.*)

MRS. GIMP: I could never keep this up. Not with my bursitis.

DOCTOR (*Moves in on* MR. GIMP): See, we are your friends. Wouldn't you like to be a man and not a dog? Men have lots more fun. Yes . . . they . . . doooooooo! See, a man can stand up on two legs, like this. Try it. (DOCTOR *and* MRS. GIMP *stand up.* MR. GIMP *hesitates, then stands up and barks.*) There. Isn't that better? Nobody steps on your hands. And a man can pick things up easily. See. (DOCTOR *starts to pick up paper with his teeth, then remembers, and uses hand. Puts back paper*) Try it. (MR. GIMP, *after some awkwardness, picks up paper with hand and then puts it in his teeth.*) (*To* MRS. GIMP) Well, little by little. We mustn't rush him. I had a patient who thought he was an eagle. I worked with him a few days, but I rushed him. He reverted. One day he tried to fly out the window. Landed on the sidewalk two stories below.

MRS. GIMP: But why didn't you *stop* him?

DOCTOR (*Thoughtfully*): He was very convincing. I thought he could make it. (*Turns to* MR. GIMP) See. He's standing on two legs, anyway. That's a start. Now, you take him home and treat him gently. No more dog food. No bones. He'll just bury them. And then . . . (MRS. GIMP *has taken her husband's paw . . . hand, that is . . . and he is walking with her, awkwardly, but erect. At this point* SMYRNA *comes clucking in, waving her hands, hopping about, making chicken sounds. She rests on a chair a moment, and then gets up, cackles, and goes out again.*)

MRS. GIMP: Who's that?

DOCTOR: That's my wife, Smyrna.

MRS. GIMP: She acts as if she thinks she is a chicken.

DOCTOR: Yes. She's been that way a year.

MRS. GIMP: But, Doctor, you're a man who is supposed to cure personality problems. I would think it would be terribly bad publicity to have a wife who thinks she's a chicken. Couldn't you cure her?

DOCTOR: Oh, yes. Certainly.

MRS. GIMP: Well, for heaven's sake, why don't you?

DOCTOR (*Moves over to chair and picks up object*): I'm selfish, I guess. (*Holds out an egg from the chair*) I'm just *crazy* about her new-laid eggs. (*He is silent a moment. Looks at* MR. *and* MRS. GIMP *strangely. Then, proudly*) Cock-a-DOODLE-dooooo! (*Curtain*)

THE END

NO STARCH IN THE COLLARS

A great many of us are convinced that what happens in laundries is not entirely a matter of chance. The buttons keep coming off too often for that.

❖ ❖ ❖ ❖ ❖

Characters
KIRK RYAN, *owner of the Determined Laundry and a proud, hard man*
ROSE
BOBBI
ELLIE
JOAN

AT RISE: *The girls are sitting nervously in chairs.* KIRK RYAN *comes in. The girls jump up and stand at attention.* RYAN *goes by and gives them an army inspection. Then he goes to the desk, waving to the girls to sit down. He sounds an "A".*

GIRLS (*Singing or chanting*):

Hail to the Determined Laundry
Established eighteen eighty-four,
Beloved Determined Laundry
Hail! And hail once more.
Hail again, that makes it three,
Hail dear Laundry, hail to thee!

(*The girls salute and sit down.*)

RYAN: I suppose you wonder why I have gathered you here together today when I should be out playing golf. The reason is simple. Your work lacks a spark. (*He holds up a package with a shirt in it. He removes the shirt.*) Look at this! This is the sort of work that will make us the laughingstock of all other laundries. Rose, name one of the traditions of laundries.

ROSE (*Hesitantly*): Uh . . . the customer always comes last.

RYAN: Ellie, could you be more specific?

ELLIE: A soft collar must always be returned starched and starched but *good!*

RYAN: Fine. Bobbi?

BOBBI: At least three wrinkles must always be pressed into the front of a good shirt.

RYAN: Excellent. Joan?

JOAN: Uh . . . well . . . the thing that makes a laundry memorable to a man is when the *tails* of the shirts are starched. This is *murder* on a hot day.

RYAN: I'm glad you thought of that. My father, who passed this beloved laundry on to me, was the inventor of uncomfortable starch in shirt tails. He always said to me, "Kirk, if you want a laundry that will make you proud, make the customer miserable." A fine old man who died at the age of ninety-seven in this very laundry, pulling buttons off shirts.

ROSE: We know everything we're supposed to do, sir.

RYAN: You know it, yes. But do you do it? No! I had a customer call up this morning and compliment us because his buttons were intact, and the inside of his collar was clean. This must *stop*.

ELLIE: What do you want us to do?

68

RYAN: You know the regulations. Come up here. If you girls continue this neatness and foolish interest in what the *customer* wants, you will be stripped of your merit badges, your seniority and your cha-cha lessons. If we are going to have fringe benefits, I want to see some fringe on the cuffs. (ELLIE *has reached the desk.* RYAN *shows her the shirt.*) What is this?

ELLIE: A shirt. An expensive, custom-made shirt. It is carefully ironed and folded neatly. The cuffs . . . the French cuffs . . . are pressed properly . . . the inside of the collar is immaculate.

RYAN: Disgusting, isn't it? Come here . . . the rest of you. Regard this work and be ashamed. I'm not mentioning who did it. I don't want any of you to have sleepless nights. Let the shame and the misery be anonymous. In fact I don't even know who owns this shirt. Now, Joan, let us start with making a perfect product to return to the average, ignorant, nasty customer . . . the normal Good Joe who always wants a refund of a dollar because he claims he sent more shirts than we returned.

BOBBI: And he usually did.

RYAN: He isn't supposed to remember. That's cheating. That's another thing I meant to bring up. When we get laundry from a man, what do we do?

ROSE: We had that in the first lesson with colored movies. We're supposed to lose one sock, at least.

ELLIE: Put starch in the cotton socks.

BOBBI: Especially the toes. . . .

JOAN: Lose three handkerchiefs, tear the monogram off one and twist one in a knot.

RYAN: What if there is a big, black note sent with the package, saying "NO STARCH"?

69

BOBBI: We put plenty of starch in everything, including the collars of T-shirts.

RYAN: Good! But none of you has followed through. Do you girls realize the Ryan Medal for Ghastly Laundry Handling has not been given in *three* years? It has not been given because none of you has deserved it.

ELLIE (*Almost in tears*): And we all took the Laundry Workers' Oath!

JOAN (*Sadly*): Yes. "I promise to do my duty to Mr. Ryan, my country and the Melodious Starch Company, to return laundry in as horrible a condition as possible and always to consider the customer as a member of an inferior race."

BOBBI: Even if he pays cash.

RYAN: Especially if he pays cash. People who pay cash can't afford credit. (*Pause*) You girls are a disgrace.

ELLIE: What can we do to be saved?

RYAN: I will give you one last lesson . . . one last chance. Come closer. Rose, take this shirt and see what can be done. (ROSE *takes the shirt, looks at it carefully, takes scissors from her pocket and cuts gay fringe in the French cuffs. Then she turns them backwards and makes X's on them with lipstick. The others ad lib remarks of praise:* "Marvelous!" "Why didn't I think of that?" *etc.*)

ROSE: *There!* Now let me see. . . .

RYAN: Don't be selfish. Let Bobbi try. (BOBBI *looks the shirt over, cuts fringe in the collar, tears off the pocket, waves the shirt around, throws it on the floor. They all jump up and down on it.*)

BOBBI (*Nastily*): That'll show you . . . you. . . .

RYAN: Don't get carried away. Give Ellie a chance. (ELLIE *takes shirt, dusts the desk top with it, dusts the walls and floor, finally cuts a little hole in the tail and sticks her nose through it. They all laugh.* ELLIE *drops the shirt on the floor and kicks it up in the air.* JOAN *catches it.*)

JOAN: I never hated a shirt so much! (*She takes scissors and cuts all the buttons off, ties the two sleeves in a knot and tosses it to* RYAN.)

RYAN (*Slowly unfolding the shirt and then trying to stuff it into laundry box for return*): I'm proud of you all. There are tears in my eyes. Down deep in your hearts you *know* how to work in a laundry. You've just been careless. I . . . I . . . (*He pauses, holds up the shirt which now looks more like a flag of truce with holes shot through it*) I . . . (*He flattens out shirt and looks at back of collar carefully*) I . . . you . . . (*He pauses. Then he turns to girls in a rage*) What's the matter with you girls? Are you crazy? What have you done? This is *my shirt!* (*He takes off the shirt he is wearing*) My *best* shirt! (*He pulls on the tattered shirt. He looks pathetic. The girls start to tiptoe out.* RYAN *stares at his shirt and then buries his head in his arms and sobs. The girls rush out. Curtain.*)

THE END

A MATTER OF TASTE

This skit takes place in a kitchen. There is a large pot on the stove, or else we will all have to imagine there is.

❖ ❖ ❖ ❖ ❖

Characters
ZELDA, *a domineering young wife, to hear tell of it*
FLO, *a young woman coming to visit her*
STELLE, *another one (neither of these guests is above some comments on her hostess)*
ANN, *a third member of the club who hates to gossip, but . . .*

AT RISE: ZELDA *looks out of the window, and then at her watch.*

ZELDA (*To herself*): My goodness! It's later than I thought. (*She takes off an apron hastily and tosses it into a corner.*) The Civic Association officers are meeting here. I told them we could all sit around the kitchen since the rest of the house is being painted. (*Goes to stove and stirs, then goes to window and calls*) Yoo-hoo, girls. Make yourselves at home. I'll be with you in a minute. (*She goes out. FLO, STELLE and ANN come in. They sniff.*)
FLO: Smells funny.

STELLE: Herring for lunch.

ANN: With raw onion and curry powder.

FLO: No. It must be the painters. Zelda's having the house done all over.

STELLE: She just had it done *last* year.

ANN: It's a mania with her. I mean, shifting the furniture around every month is all right . . .

STELLE: Yes. And new curtains and slip covers every season are understandable.

FLO: Sure. And a few dozen new plants every month are nice. But not redecorating and cleaning every time you turn around.

STELLE: It's her poor husband I feel sorry for. They say she makes him go down in the cellar to smoke.

ANN: I don't mean to gossip, but I've been told her husband has to take his shoes off before he comes in the house.

FLO: Well, I'm not one to pass on stories but they say she makes him wear gloves around the house so he won't get dirty fingerprints on the white woodwork.

STELLE: How did she ever get to be president of our Civic Association?

ANN: The mayor's her uncle.

FLO: The chief of police is her second cousin.

STELLE: I'll bet she'll come down here with a hat on and long white gloves.

FLO: That's her idea of being informal.

ANN: She's really a good egg, though. I mean if she didn't *talk* so much.

STELLE: I understand she's an atrocious cook. Not that I want to run her down. She makes a good president. You don't have to ask her to speak up.

ANN: Sometimes you want to ask her to *shut* up.

FLO: She has a lot of good points. She gave fifty dollars to the Association last year.

STELLE: Sure. She was the treasurer.

ANN: I wonder if she really *does* starve her husband. I know *she's* always on a diet. (*Edges toward the boiling pot*)

STELLE: She claims she takes size ten.

FLO: She takes *two* size tens. Not that I want to be mean.

ANN (*Pointing to pot*): I wonder what she's cooking.

STELLE (*Goes over and sniffs*): Smells interesting. But then, I'm hungry.

FLO (*Takes a ladle and dips it in, then sips from it. Stops thoughtfully, sips some more*): Hmnnnnnn.

STELLE (*Takes ladle and sips*): Beet soup . . . borscht . . . something like that.

ANN (*Takes ladle and sips*): Something besides beets in it. Something subtle.

STELLE: Needs salt. (*She puts a little salt in it.*)

ANN: A dash of curry seems called for.

FLO: Nutmeg wouldn't hurt. (*They toss "spices" in and then taste it in turn*)

STELLE: It's getting there. Some sliced onion, maybe. (*Pretends to open refrigerator and find onion. Starts slicing*)

FLO: I noticed some leftover halibut. That should give it a tang. (*Pretends to open refrigerator and crumble fish into pot*)

ANN (*Tasting*): It does take away that *odd* taste. (*She opens refrigerator and looks around*) What about some raw hamburg and some seedless grapes?

STELLE (*At refrigerator*): We'll give Zelda's husband a really nourishing stew tonight. Here's an old bunch of carrots.

ANN (*Helping her*): And some hard cheese.

FLO: Ooooh. That sounds good. (*She reaches up to an imaginary shelf and takes a bottle*) Just a dash of white wine. (*Pours*)

ANN (*Tastes*): Real yummy. What an improvement!

FLO (*Tastes*): Delicious. It would cost you three dollars in a restaurant.

STELLE (*Tasting*): Still has an odd basic flavor, though. Awfully good, however. Imagine, with some good sour rye bread.

FLO: Shhhh. Here comes Zelda. (STELLE *still has the ladle to her mouth when* ZELDA *comes in.* ZELDA *stares at her in surprise.*)

STELLE: We took the liberty of adding a few ingredients.

ZELDA: Ingredients?

FLO: Yes. We put in some carrots and fish and stuff. Improves it.

ZELDA: Carrots? Fish? But . . .

ANN: Yes. As beet soup, it had a strange taste.

ZELDA (*Aghast*): That's not beet soup. (*She puts ladle in and brings out crimson kitchen curtains*) Here are my kitchen curtains. I'm dyeing them red! (*Curtain*)

THE END

ANDROCLES AND HIS PAL

This is the true story of Androcles and the Lion, taken from an ancient manuscript nobody can read; thus, it is obviously authentic. In order to put on this historical sketch it is not necessary to have a lion. It is not even necessary to have a lion suit since tailors are reluctant to make them—and anyhow, a lion suit seldom fits. The tail always seems out of place and there are no change pockets. Any gifted young man can get down on his haunches, roar, and slap his hands around like paws. If he can get someone to hang a sign on him saying LION, that should convince nearly everyone. We also have a chimpanzee in here which does not appear in the usual story but is vouched for by the old manuscript. A real chimp is not necessary, either. A chimp is anybody who lets his long arms hang, beats his breast, and would rather walk on all fours than upright.

❖ ❖ ❖ ❖ ❖

Characters
ANDROCLES, *a Roman slave*
LION, *a lion*
CHIMP, *a chimpanzee*
SOLDIER, *a Roman soldier*

AT RISE: *The* LION *is sitting on his haunches on a path in the woods. He is wailing. A* CHIMP *enters, walking upright.*

CHIMP: Hey, Lion. Is it necessary to make such a noise? We chimpanzees are trying to have a quiet game of Monopoly.

LION: I guess I'm the King of Beasts. I guess I can wail if I like.

CHIMP: O.K. So you're the King of Beasts. There's never been a democratic election, but suit yourself.

LION (*Roaring*): You know what happens to people who start that? Chimpanzees, especially? (*Goes back to wailing and looking at his foot*) Oh, my foot, my foot! I've never felt such pain.

CHIMP: You want I should call Dr. Giraffe? Or Dr. Kildare?

LION: I am beyond doctors. I need someone who can extract a thorn.

CHIMP: I can do it, but I'll need tweezers.

LION: I can't wait. What's the use of being King of the Beasts when I sit here in pain? I need a specialist.

CHIMP: How did you get the thorn?

LION (*Wails, thrashes around, roars;* CHIMP *jumps back*): Picking roses. How do you think?

CHIMP: Now you're being funny.

LION: There's nothing funny about this. The Romans tried me out for eating slaves in the Colosseum. I had to work out in a rose garden. They signed me up, and I'm supposed to be in Rome tomorrow or I lose the job.

CHIMP: Oh, Lion, King of Beasts! What's so hot about chewing up slaves in Rome?

LION: It's the glory of the thing. New faces. Thousands cheering. It's like the Rose Bowl. I'm an all-star lion and thousands will cheer.

CHIMP: What if the slave beats you?

LION: So you go hungry that day.

CHIMP: Sounds exciting. They don't use chimpanzees, do they?

LION: Ho, ho! Who ever heard of throwing slaves to the chimpanzees?

CHIMP: I was just *asking*.

LION: A lion lives in the best of dens . . . split-level, with his own swimming pool—Roman bath, that is. He has his own barber, and all the slaves he can catch. Believe me, it's not like this jungle life. (*Starts to wail loudly again*) Ooooh, my foot hurts.

CHIMP (*Pointing*): Here comes a human being. Human beings can pull out thorns.

LION: Sure, but we've given ourselves a bad name with them.

CHIMP: Now and then you run into one who understands animals.

LION: Not very often. Does this human being have a spear?

CHIMP: No. Just a slave costume. (*Pause*) I'll ask him, anyway. Don't roar, whatever you do. (ANDROCLES *appears, hesitates, gets as far away from the animals as possible.* CHIMP *goes up to him.*) Pardon me, sir.

ANDROCLES: I'm not a sir. I'm a plain slave, and the Romans are looking for me. I forgot to punch out last Friday.

CHIMP: I am a poor chimpanzee. I have a friend in trouble.

ANDROCLES: I have to be on my way. I'll get caught. Who's your friend?

CHIMP: A friendly, good-natured, intelligent lion—a lover of string quartets, Mozart, things like that.

ANDROCLES: A lion! (*He jumps away.*) No! *No!*

CHIMP: A very decent sort of lion, not the common run of lions. Quite a jolly chap, really.

ANDROCLES: I'm sorry. I have to go. They'll catch me.

CHIMP: Have you no compassion, no pity, no feeling?

ANDROCLES: Oh, all right. Where's the lion?

CHIMP: Right here. (*He pulls* ANDROCLES *to* LION)

LION (*Roaring, and then wailing*): Oh, I am in distress. I am in pain. Help me and I will never forget.

ANDROCLES (*Moves toward the* LION *cautiously*): What's your name, Lion?

LION: Leo. I have a thorn in my paw.

ANDROCLES: This isn't a stickup, is it?

LION: Never. This is on the level. See? My paw? (*Holds up paw*)

ANDROCLES (*Looking at paw*): It does look sore.

CHIMP: He's in great pain.

ANDROCLES: O.K. Let me have your paw. (*Takes paw*) Hm-m-m. Very sore. Now, steady. This may hurt a bit. (*He pulls and twists while the* LION *wails and the* CHIMP *jumps up and down in sympathy. At last the thorn comes out.*)

LION: It's out! Oh, how can I thank you? Why, I don't even know your name.

ANDROCLES: My name is Androcles.

LION: Androcles! A noble name. Oh, my paw feels so much better.

ANDROCLES: I have to go. Take two aspirin, if the paw hurts. And bathe it in Epsom salts regularly to take down the swelling. (*A* SOLDIER *suddenly enters.*)

SOLDIER: Hey, Androcles. Halt! I have you now. (ANDROCLES *runs off with* SOLDIER *running after him.*)

CURTAIN

* * * *

Scene Two takes place in the Roman Colosseum. (*There is a sign that says so.*) It is a few days later.

AT RISE: *The* LION *is prowling around the arena. (Off-stage, if possible, people should be yelling.) He rises and bows once or twice, gets down again, and roars. Finally, he speaks to audience.*

LION: You don't know how this is, friends. They starve you so that when you get out here in the Roman Colosseum with a slave, all you think of is dinner. It's not the racket they made it out to be. It's the old saying, "When in Rome, don't trust the Romans." (SOLDIER *enters with* ANDROCLES. *He leaves* ANDROCLES *standing at side and goes to center.*)

SOLDIER: This is the final bout of the evening. The middle-weight championship of the lions. This bout will be fought to a decision. On my right, Leo, King of Beasts, weighing in at three-fifty-two—and that sounds over-weight, but that's how it goes. Wearing brown tights, Leo, winner of ten successive bouts with slaves. (*Cheers are heard from offstage*) On my left, shaking in his slave's boots, is Androcles, weighing in at one-fifty-six, and wearing slave's tights. This is Androcles' first bout, and probably his last. Because this is an *elimination* tournament, if you know what I mean. Winner takes all. Ha, ha, ha. (*Beckons to* LION) Come here, champ. (*He brings* LION *and* ANDROCLES *together at center.* LION *sits down, holds up "paw." They shake hands.* SOLDIER *puts boxing gloves on* LION *and* ANDROCLES.) Now, you both under-stand the rules. After a knockdown, you retire to a neu-tral corner. And no punching in the clinches, see? O.K. Come out fighting. (SOLDIER *backs away and the* LION *gets down on all fours and starts roaring and nipping at* ANDROCLES, *who backs away.* LION *stands up and gets close to* ANDROCLES)

LION (*Whispers*): I'm your old pal, Leo.

ANDROCLES (*Puzzled*): Leo? Oh, Leo. The thorn. In the woods.

LION: I'm starving, Andy. But I'll spare you. You have nothing to worry about. (*Socks* ANDROCLES *hard*) That's just to make it look legal.

ANDROCLES: Fancy meeting *you* here. (*He is boxing gently all the time.*)

LION: I never forget a favor. You have nothing to worry about. You will be a hero. The first slave to beat a lion in Roman history. Now, pretend you're afraid for a while and then you can knock me out. (LION *gets down on all fours, roars and chases* ANDROCLES *around awhile.*)

ANDROCLES: Get up and fight, you bum. (LION *gets up and boxes for a while, foolishly. Finally* ANDROCLES *socks him and he falls with a mild roar.* SOLDIER *counts to ten, raises* ANDROCLES' *hand.*)

SOLDIER: The winner, and first slave ever to beat a lion. In the first round, Androcles. The new champion! You will be granted any favor you wish. (*The* LION *gets up and roars weakly and waddles around.*)

ANDROCLES: I want the lion to be sent back to his natural home in the jungle. He put up a good fight. He just didn't train enough, I guess.

SOLDIER: Would you care to say a few words for the Rome *Daily News?*

ANDROCLES: Well, I guess I was lucky. I got him with a left hook. Of course, I've always led a good clean slave's life, and I never smoke. And I want to thank my mother for her faith in me. And I just want to say I think the lion put up a good fight.

SOLDIER: Are you going to have a rematch?

ANDROCLES: No, after this I'm going to retire. I'll probably

81

get some acting contracts and some chariot racing spots . . . I expect I'll be promoted to a citizen, and possibly I'll open a bowling alley. That's about all, I guess. (*Curtain*)

THE END

HOW THE WEST WAS LOST

This skit takes place on a street in Gold Gulch City in the Old West. Yippee! There is a sign that says: MAIN STREET, *and, to the left, another sign that says:* JOE'S PLACE, NO DANCING WITH YOUR SPURS ON. *To the right there is a sign with a directional arrow that says:* TO NEW YORK— SCENIC ROUTE. *Anything else in the way of cowboy scenery and costumes is that much velvet. Or leather.*

❖ ❖ ❖ ❖ ❖

Characters
GAMBLING JOE, *a gambler and owner of a dance hall*
BANKER TOM, *a banker and owner of nearly everything else*
SHERIFF TATE, *a cowardly sheriff with good intentions*
FALLING ROCKS, *an Indian, brother of Deer Crossing*
DESPERATE BILLY, *a ruthless desperado with a weakness*

AT RISE: SHERIFF TATE *enters. He is very nervous. He keeps looking around, checking behind, to the sides, etc. He takes a gun from a holster or pocket, looks at it nervously, drops it with shaking hands, picks it up, and takes a deep breath.*

83

SHERIFF (*To himself*): I must be brave. Gold Gulch City depends on me. That's why they elected me Sheriff. That . . . and the fact that Desperate Billy shot all the other candidates dead. Billy always had an alibi. He could always prove he was shooting someone else in Dodge City at the time. (*He takes a deep breath and straightens up, then twirls his gun casually and takes a few cowboy steps. He starts talking to an imaginary desperado.*) Now lookee here, Desperate Billy. I'm not going to allow your kind in Gold Gulch City. You come down this here Main Street at high noon, and you'll meet *me*. . . . (*Stops, takes a paper from his pocket, reads it, puts it back*) and you'll meet *me* . . . Lightning Tate, the fastest draw west of the Pecos. I draw so fast and shoot so fast, I've shot three pairs of shoes off my own feet 'cause I cain't get out of the way quick enough. (*He stops suddenly, pretends to shoot, smiles happily.*) I had to do it, Billy. It was me or you. And better you than me. I'm not forgetting how crazy you are about girls . . . I'm not forgetting how you stole my one true love from me . . . my Betty Lou . . . nor how you stole my other true love from me, Nancy Ann . . . nor how you stole all my other *one* true loves from me, like Sally Jane and Brigitte Liz. (GAMBLING JOE *comes on. He stares at the* SHERIFF *a moment.*)

JOE: You better come in outen from that hot sun, Sheriff Tate. (*At the sound of* JOE's *voice, the* SHERIFF *trembles, drops his gun and picks it up again nervously.*)

SHERIFF: Oh, it's you, Gambling Joe. It's near high noon and Desperate Billy'll soon be coming; rootin', tootin' and a-shootin'.

JOE: Waal. His rootin' and his tootin' aren't so bad . . . but I guess we're all plumb scared of his shootin'. (*He comes to the* SHERIFF.) I believe in calling a spade a spade.

SHERIFF: I know that. You nearly shot me because I called a spade a club playing poker with you last night.

JOE: No. I got mad because you weren't playing the hand I *dealt* you. (*Pause*) I know you're skeered pea-green of Billy. I want to tell you about a fellow I saw in a medicine show in Tucson. He turned his back and looked at a mirror, and he shot perfectly over his shoulder.

SHERIFF: That's an idea. Billy won't even know I'm looking at him. (JOE *backs away.* SHERIFF *takes a pocket mirror out, turns his back on* JOE, *puts the revolver over his shoulder and shoots. Loud squawking of some "chickens" is heard from offstage, or a duck might fall onstage.*)

JOE: I don't think you have the hang of it, Sheriff. (BANKER TOM *comes on. He nods to the* SHERIFF *and* JOE.)

TOM: I'm mighty nervous with Desperate Billy coming to town at high noon to shoot it out. I hope his watch is slow.

JOE: I couldn't sleep last night thinking about it.

TOM: Of course, if I were a trained sheriff, it wouldn't bother me none.

SHERIFF (*Shakily*): What would you do?

TOM: Don't shake so much, son. Your levis are falling down. (*Pause*) I'd walk slowly up to him as he comes to me with his gun drawn. (*He pantomimes this.*) I'd walk right up to him and look straight at his gun and I'd say, "Billy, I'm not scared of any man in the West." Then I'd grab his gun outen his hand and slap him across the face with it. (*He does this to an imaginary desperado. At the same time,* FALLING ROCKS, *an Indian, appears in front of him.* TOM *jumps and backs away.*) You scared me, Indian. Thought you was Desperate Billy.

FALLING ROCKS: Me Falling Rocks, good Indian. Ugh! How! Me beatnik Indian. Sad Sioux. Everybody in West know me. Signs everywhere: LOOK OUT FOR FALLING ROCKS.

JOE: He's not as tough as his brother, Deer Crossing. Every few miles in the West, they have *signs:* DANGER, DEER CROSSING.

FALLING ROCKS: Same thing me cousin, Winding Road.

SHERIFF: Falling Rocks, I'm going to make you a deputy to take care of Desperate Billy.

FALLING ROCKS: Who ever heard of Indian sheriff? No thankum. Me have heap big trouble just shooting rabbits.

SHERIFF (*Suddenly and very nervously*):Hark!

TOM: Hark? Is that Western lingo? Hark?

SHERIFF: List! I hear him afar, singing his theme song. (*Sings*)

> "I'm Desperate Billy from Texas, hey!
> I'm rough and I'm tough and I'm durty.
> I shoot every man that gits in my way,
> But I love every lady who's purty."

FALLING ROCKS: Heap good poetry. Almost scans. (SHERIFF *walks nervously about in circles.*)

TOM: Calm down, now, Sheriff. You're not the first sheriff of Coyote County to be finished off by Billy. It won't hurt but for more'n a minute.

SHERIFF: Th-that's enough. (*He holds his head sadly.*)

JOE: Easy does it, Sheriff. Don't worry. We can probably get another sheriff.

FALLING ROCKS: Wait! Don't run. Falling Rocks gotum big idea. Billy no shootum girls. Billy likeum girls. Sheriff run in—(*He points*) to Gambling Joe's Dance Hall and

Public Library. Borrow dancing girl's clothes. Billy no shootum. (*Proudly*) Man, that's a cool idea!

Tom: That's not bad at all.

Joe: That's so smart *I* should have thought of it.

Sheriff (*Listens intently*): I can hear Desperate Billy shootin'. (*Looks at the others*) I'll do it. You all wait here and give me moral support. (*He rushes off.*)

Falling Rocks: Sheriff make good squaw. Got nice smile.

Tom: How'd he get to be sheriff anyway?

Joe: Politics. His father-in-law has influence.

Tom: Wanted to help him, huh?

Joe: No, wanted to get rid of him.

Falling Rocks: Indians vanishing race. Falling Rocks go vanish. See you around the campus. (*He goes.*)

Tom (*Listening*): Billy's getting closer.

Joe: I ought to be going myself. I have an appointment with my doctor in Phoenix to have my legs stopped from shakin'.

Tom: I have to see my dentist in Flagstaff, by rights. Stop my teeth from chatterin'.

Joe (*Nervously*): Where is the sheriff?

Tom: I also ought to see the shoemaker about the way I'm quakin' in my boots.

Billy (*Singing offstage*):

> "I'm Desperate Billy from Texas, hey!
> I love all the gals who are pretty
> I give them all rings
> And beautiful things
> I rob from the stores in the city."

Joe: Here comes Billy. I wonder where the sheriff is. (*The* Sheriff *enters, dressed as a girl—preferably a Western girl, but a girl, anyway. He walks gracefully in front of*

JOE *and* TOM, *swinging a big heavy handbag around his wrist.*)

SHERIFF (*Speaking in a falsetto*): Good morning, gentlemen. Charming varmint of a day, isn't it?

JOE (*Very politely*): Howdy, ma'am. Don't believe I've had the pleasure.

TOM: Howdy, ma'am. You're a stranger in these parts. I hope you'll allow me to show you the town. It won't take but five minutes.

SHERIFF (*In his own voice*): How do I look, fellows? I just put on an old thing I made myself.

TOM (*Pleased*): Sheriff! You look wonderful.

JOE: I never could have guessed it—although you *do* need a shave.

SHERIFF: Sh! Here . . . (*Changes to high voice*) here comes Billy. Huddle together and we'll be talking.

BILLY (*Enters holding pistols and swaggering*): Where's that no-good, good-for-nothing sheriff?

SHERIFF (*To* JOE *and* TOM, *loudly*): Who is that crude creature? He's so ugly . . . and so redundant.

BILLY: I'm after that cowardly sheriff! I'll shoot his ears off, then I'll shoot his toes off. . . .

SHERIFF: What a nasty braggart!

TOM: Miss Nellie, I think you had better withdraw to safety. A beautiful girl like you is in danger.

JOE: Yes, Miss Nellie, why not take refuge with Parson Beechcroft. Your life is not safe here. (BILLY *stands smiling at the* SHERIFF. SHERIFF *acts coy and shy, twirls big handbag around, hits himself lightly on the side of the head, nearly falls over, but* TOM *and* JOE *catch him and set him upright.*)

BILLY: Waaal, as I live and breathe, a beautiful gal. I never harm beautiful girls. I might say, ma'am, they make me forget all about shootin' and rootin' and tootin'.

TOM: You must flee, Nellie. This is Desperate Billy!

SHERIFF: He seems to be quite a gentleman.

JOE (*Introducing them*): Miss Nellie Nubbins from the East . . . Desperate Billy.

BILLY: Pleased to meet up with you. My real monicker is Percival Cunningham. But you can just call me Billy.

SHERIFF: Charmed to meet you. . . . Billy. (*Giggles flirtatiously, swings handbag about like a nervous young girl.*)

BILLY (*As* TOM *and* JOE *move away, making knowing faces at each other*): Miss Nellie, I'd be obliged if you'd take a little walk with me among the desert flowers.

SHERIFF: Oh, really, Mr. Billy, I don't know you well enough.

BILLY (*Putting his arm around* SHERIFF's *waist*): Aw, come on.

SHERIFF: You *are* handsome. (BILLY *lowers his head bashfully. The* SHERIFF *winds up and delivers, hitting* BILLY *over the head with the handbag.* BILLY *blinks a moment, swallows, whirls his head around, and then falls flat.* SHERIFF *speaks in his natural voice.*) All right, you two, take him over there and lock him in the jail. I'm the sheriff around here, and I mean business. (*He advances on* TOM *and* JOE, *twirling the handbag. They hastily take hold of* BILLY *and pull him off. The* SHERIFF *smiles proudly. He dances around and sings, falsetto.*)

"I'm brave and courageous Sheriff Tate.

Desperados are one thing I hate!"

(*He changes his stride and deepens his voice.*) I sure don't want this to be a habit. I have to learn to outshoot these desperados. (*He takes mirror, turns back to audience, points gun over his shoulder at audience. He shoots, and again the chickens are heard, or, if possible, a duck might drop down. He is disgusted. He takes up same position again.* BILLY, *showing signs of a struggle, comes on from left, gun pointed.* SHERIFF *doesn't see* BILLY. SHERIFF *shoots over shoulder in opposite direction.* BILLY *clutches heart and drops.* SHERIFF *stares, astonished, as* TOM, JOE *and* FALLING ROCKS *run in shouting happily.*)

THE END

THE WURST STUDENT

This is a romantic story in the operetta tradition that is full of heartbreak, duels, revolutions, and stuff. The fragments of songs will fit some Viennese waltz or other, or you can make up your own schmaltzy tunes as you go along. The scene is Papa Lopchick's root beer garden which caters to students of Old Wiener Schnitzel Military Academy. There might be a sign saying: WELCOME, STUDENTS OF OLD WIENER SCHNITZEL. NO DUELING DURING DESSERT.

❖ ❖ ❖ ❖ ❖

Characters
PAPA LOPCHICK, *the owner of a root beer garden*
KITTI, *a pretty waitress (but not pretty enough)*
HANS, *a handsome cadet*
FRITZ, *another one*
EMPEROR FRANZ OTTO, *an emperor*

AT RISE: KITTI *is straightening a table.* PAPA *is looking around nervously.* KITTI *puts down a plate one way,* PAPA *changes it.* KITTI *places a root beer mug at one side,* PAPA *changes it to another. They bump into each other now and then.*

PAPA: You do not have experience as a waitress?
KITTI: Nein. I once dressed the hair for beautiful duchesses.

PAPA: Now you will dress the pigs' feet. (*Looks at watch*) Ach! Three o'clock. Soon will come the noisy, fighting students from Old Wiener Schnitzel.

KITTI: Such brave, strong men. Ah, Vienna, city of light and bravery. (*She starts to waltz around by herself and falls over a chair. She gets up and stares off.*) Here they come! The brave cadets.

PAPA: The bums! (KITTI *rushes off.* HANS *and* FRITZ *come on, laughing and patting each other on the back. They have swords or reasonable facsimiles*) Ah, brave students of Old Wiener Schnitzel, what is the joke?

HANS: Who knows, Papa? We are young and brave, and it is good to laugh.

FRITZ: It was a limerick.

> "There was an old man from Peru,
> Who dreamed he was kissing his shoe.
> He woke in the night
> In a terrible fright
> To find it was perfectly true."

(*They all laugh heartily,* HANS *and* FRITZ *banging each other on the back and also banging poor* PAPA, *who finally collapses as* KITTI *comes in with two mugs of root beer. She tries to help* PAPA *up, but "spills" root beer on him.*)

KITTI: Ach! I give Papa a bath in root beer. (*She rushes out.*)

PAPA (*Rising and blinking*): The Danube is overflowing. (*This starts the boys laughing and banging again.* PAPA *gets quickly out of the way.* KITTI *comes in again with two mugs, puts them on the table. The cadets sit down and raise their glasses.*)

HANS: To our Emperor Franz Otto!

FRITZ: To our emperor!

HANS: Ah, if I were only of the royal blood. I would ride white horses and do tricks. (*He waves his glass about and* PAPA *gets more liquid in the face.*)

FRITZ: Ah, if I were of the royal blood, I would sleep in a velvet bed and eat hot dogs for breakfast.

PAPA: Wieners.

KITTI: Ah, brave cadets of Old Wiener Schnitzel! I salute you. I came here to work because I am so proud of you.

HANS: We are proud of us, too. (*Sings or chants*)

> To Old Wiener Schnitzel
> Always full of good cheer.
> Where the days of our youth
> Are spent being uncouth.
> In Old Wiener Schnitzel.
> In Old Wiener Schnitzel.

KITTI: Pum-pum. Pum-pum.

PAPA: Where they use swords and spears
          Like the three Musketeers——

KITTI: And to music and cheers
          They become brigadiers.

BOYS: In old, Old Wiener Schnitzel!

PAPA: Und where is Cadet Popoff today?

HANS: He lost his head. Dueling.

PAPA: Ah, what a brave scar he will have!

FRITZ: But no head, alas.

PAPA: And noble Cadet Wilhelm?

HANS: He lost his leg in a duel.

PAPA: Such low dueling?

FRITZ: His opponent was using a scythe.

KITTI: Ah, you brave, foolish, manly boys!

FRITZ: More root beer, fraulein. We are men who like to be waited on immediately.

KITTI (*Comes to front and speaks aside to the audience*):

Little do they know I am of the royal blood. I am here incognito. (*She goes out.* FRITZ *picks up a glove and slaps* HANS *on the face.*)

HANS: That *hurt.* (*He takes the glove and slaps* FRITZ.)

PAPA: No fights here. The emperor often comes for kraut mit horse und pepper. (FRITZ *and* HANS *each take a glove and slap* PAPA. *They laugh and carry on.* PAPA *now turns away, wounded, and walks to front, speaks in an aside*) Ach! Little do they know I am of the royal blood. Only because I wish to study the cadets do I remain here incognito for thirty-two years. Besides, I have no *proof* I am of the royal blood, except a certificate my dying mother left me, that said: "Royal Laundry." (KITTI *comes in with two glasses of root beer and places them on the table for the boys. She stands there.*)

FRITZ (*To* HANS): I slapped your face. That means a duel if you have any pride and courage.

HANS: Cool, man, cool.

FRITZ: Coward!

HANS: No one can call me a coward without fighting to the death. . . . except you.

KITTI (*To* HANS): Coward! You are a disgrace to the Austrian Empire.

HANS (*Rises and walks to the front. Speaks in an aside to the audience*): Little do they know I am of the royal blood, attending Old Wiener Schnitzel incognito. It is forbidden by the emperor to duel with the students. I am too good. (*He goes back and sits down, drinking his root beer.*)

PAPA (*To* HANS): The emperor shall hear of this. You shall be stripped of your medals, your dress uniform, your horse and your red-white-and-black underwear embroidered with the Imperial Eagle. (*They all turn suddenly to the rear. Nothing happens.*)

HANS: We turned too quickly. Let's try it again. (*They all turn suddenly and* EMPEROR FRANZ OTTO *comes in. They all bow and then the cadets salute.*)

FRITZ: Our beloved emperor.

HANZ: Our noble emperor.

EMPEROR: Skip it, kids. I am no longer your emperor.

PAPA: A revolution? So early in the day?

KITTI: Our noble emperor who can do the Viennese waltz, the lancers, the twist and the cha-cha?

EMPEROR: Emperor no more.

HANS: No more? The noble Franz Otto, who batted .412 in the Balkan League last year?

EMPEROR: My grandmother is dying. She sent me a message. She is not my grandmother. I am not the heir to the throne. I never was. I was stolen from my mother and placed in the palace in the crib of the real emperor who was put on the doorstep of the Royal Laundry. The true emperor is Papa.

PAPA: I *knew* it. I knew it!

FRITZ: Then I am the Crown Prince!

HANS: And I am your cousin and Papa's son!

EMPEROR: All too true.

KITTI (*To* PAPA): Then I . . . *I* must be your mother! And I am twenty-five years younger than you are.

EMPEROR: Only in old Vienna could this happen. Only in the land of Old Wiener Schnitzel Academy! (*He sings*)
>
> In Old Wiener Schnitzel
> Nothing's ever quite clear
> Royal blood may, I fear,
> Overnight disappear.

BOYS:	In Old Wiener Schnitzel.
	In Old Wiener Schnitzel.
PAPA:	Oh, one day he's a king
	With a crown glitt-er-*ing*
	And the next, ding-a-ling
	He's not a darn thing!
KITTI:	In a pinch
	You can clinch
	Your hold on the throne.
	It's a cinch
	They can lynch
	You next day and postpone—
FRITZ:	All your laughter,
	Hereafter,
HANS:	And just leave you alone.
EMPEROR:	In Old Wiener Schnitzel,
	In Old Wiener Schnitzel.
	With the clamor and glamor,
	Romance and root beer.
PAPA:	Since I'm the real king,
	Though it doesn't mean a thing,
	I can say, without fear
	That I'm so glad I'm here.

ALL: Give Old Wiener Schnitzel a che-e-e-er! (*They all bow to* PAPA *who bows, too, bumps his head against* FRITZ's *head and faints.* KITTI *pours root beer on him as they cheer.*)

ALL: Long live the Emperor!

THE END

WHERE BANKING IS A PLEASURE

This skit takes place in the office of the president of the Fifth National Bank. A desk and chair are necessary, and something that resembles a phone and intercom. If possible, there should be signs about: FIFTH NATIONAL BANK: FIRST IN CHEERFULNESS! . . . IF YOU NEED MONEY, WE HAVE IT. . . . WE LEND MONEY WITH A SMILE, SOMETIMES WITH A LAUGH.

❖ ❖ ❖ ❖ ❖

Characters

HARLAN PEPPERSTALL, *a big-hearted banker with high ideals and interest rates, president of Fifth National*

JIM CUBBY, *a reporter*

MRS. KONK, *a borrower*

HOMER JOBBLE, *another borrower, a bit wilder in his aims*

TONY, *the bank's barber*

MISS CUDDLE, *the bank's entertainer-in-residence*

BILL, *a lowly bookkeeper*

SLUGGER, *one of the bank's special officers*

AT RISE: HARLAN PEPPERSTALL *sits at his desk, and listens to his intercom.*

HARLAN: Yes, yes. Send that reporter in. The president of the Fifth National Bank is always happy to meet the press. (*He gets up, goes over to what would be a full-length mirror. Looks himself over. Combs his hair. Looks sideways to try to see profile. Returns to desk. Takes stage money or something similar out of drawer, makes piles on desk, plays with it, etc.* JIM CUBBY *comes in.*)

JIM: I'm Jim Cubby of the *Morning Globe.*

HARLAN: Sit down. This is the bank with the wall-to-wall money. I am the man who lends it with a smile. (*He dribbles the money through his hands.*)

JIM: Yes, sir. We know that. I was thinking of dressing you up like Santa Claus and taking your picture. We'd run a little story about your bank . . . how it just can't wait to loan money . . . how it really doesn't care if you *never* pay it back.

HARLAN (*Clears throat*): Except that the law forces us to make you pay it back. (*Pause*) Alas! (*Pause*) Santa Claus, eh?

JIM: Everybody knows you're the Santa Claus of this city, . . . you're always so kind and eager and determined to loan money. . . .

HARLAN (*Nodding*): Not a bad idea. I'll have my tailor make me a single-breasted Santa Claus suit with stretch pants and a beard to match.

JIM: Good. I'll call you up in a week or so, and then I'll make an appointment with the photographer.

HARLAN: Fine. (*Pause*) You're sure you don't need any money?

JIM: No, thank you. Like all newspaper reporters, I am vastly *overpaid!* (JIM *picks up a bill.*) I'll just take a small sample to show my friends. (*He goes out quickly.*

HARLAN *stares after him with an annoyed frown. He goes back to mirror, looks himself over. Practices "Ho, ho, ho!" etc. Door opens and* HARLAN *goes back to desk as* MRS. KONK, *a bird-like woman with a piping voice, comes in.*)

MRS. KONK: Good afternoon. I'm Mrs. Konk. Remember me? Ooooh, I'm so thrilled. It isn't often I talk to a bank president. Have you ever thought of starting a fan club?

HARLAN: Sit down and be calm, Mrs. Konk. Fan club? Well, many of our borrowers who are aware of my modesty, my generosity, my virtue, my vision, my wisdom *and* my natural charm have wanted to form a fan club. But I believe it would be undignified. I think our customers are happy enough with free balloons, lollipops, Green Stamps, candy canes, pony rides and thermal undershirts. (*Sits down*) And what is *your* pleasure, Mrs. Konk? This month, with each loan, we are adding a set of genuine English bone chinaware made from indestructible translucent plastic.

MRS. KONK: I hate to mention it, but I've been *so* extravagant since you made me the last loan . . .

HARLAN: Good. Keeps the economy thriving. Live beyond your means, and keep America free!

MRS. KONK: You remember I borrowed four thousand dollars for a new car? Well, two trees and a guard rail ran into it.

HARLAN: The mayor ought to do something about that. But don't worry. The car probably needed washing and greasing. Simpler to buy a new one. Why not take *ten* thousand dollars and buy *two* new ones? Why not make it *thirty* thousand and buy a new house, *too?*

MRS. KONK: I could use a new house. The old one needs painting.

HARLAN (*Takes a piece of paper, scribbles something*): Just sign this and give it to the teller. He'll credit your account with thirty thousand dollars less sixteen thousand interest and give you Green Stamps, lollipops, plastic cups and a Smokey the Bear hat.

MRS. KONK (*Signing slip*): I suppose I'll have to pay it all back some day?

HARLAN: Why worry? Take forty years to pay. It's only money.

MRS. KONK: Thank you so much. You're a *good* man. (*She goes out as* HOMER JOBBLE *comes in.*)

HARLAN (*Looks at paper*): Mr. Jobble?

HOMER: Call me Homer. I need money. I throw it away. Burns a hole in my pocket. Never can save a nickel.

HARLAN: I like people who throw money away. It keeps the economy at a high level.

HOMER: I buy crazy stuff on the installment plan. Bought an ocean liner last month, complete with staff, life belts and shuffleboard. (*Pulls on imaginary cap, goes "Toooot, tooooot!" "Women and children first!" "Man overboard!" "Batten down the hatches!"*)

HARLAN: Splendid. Without installment buying, people would have to be satisfied with what they could *afford*. Now billions of dollars are spent on things we *can't* afford and the economy is booming! Be patriotic! Get in debt and stay in debt!

HOMER: I also paid a few thousand dollars for advance cha-cha lessons. Look! (*Does some cha-cha steps, pretending he has a teacher with him*) Beautiful stuff!

HARLAN: Money well spent. How much do you want?

HOMER: Ten thousand, twenty thousand. . . . (*He sits.*)

HARLAN: That doesn't seem *enough* for a man of your tastes. Take thirty thousand and get a free trip to Sun

Valley. (*Talks into intercom*) Hello, Main Floor Entertainment Area? Miss Flugle? . . . She's dancing with one of the customers in the vault? Good. . . . How about Miss Cuddle? Just finished her act in the Christmas Club window? . . . Fine. Have her send Tony in, and come in herself. (*To* HOMER) We like to keep our customers entertained and amused. (MISS CUDDLE *comes in.*) Ah, Miss Cuddle. (MISS CUDDLE *can be any kind of entertainer you prefer. She should wear an elaborate costume, and have some kind of instrument.*) I hope you won't mind entertaining Mr. Jobble while he thinks about a loan. (MISS CUDDLE *smiles and goes into her act. In a moment,* TONY *comes in. He should wear a white jacket and carry a comb and scissors.*)

TONY: You wish some hairs remodeled, Mr. Pepperstall?

HARLAN: Yes, Tony. Give Mr. Jobble a light trim while he thinks about borrowing some money. (HOMER *leans back.* TONY *pretends to be giving him a trim, standing back and gazing artistically at the creation now and then.* HARLAN *speaks into intercom.*) Charlie? What's Percy doing? . . . Watering the fresh fig tree on the mezzanine? Well, have him come in here and give a customer a shoe shine. Eh? . . . Oh, passing out candy apples and soap bubble sets. Well, don't disturb him. (*To* HOMER) Well? Do you want the money? I'll throw in a one-way trip to Pago Pago.

HOMER: How will I get back to pay you?

HARLAN (*Quickly*): Hmm. I'll make it a round-trip.

HOMER: That's better. (*To* TONY) Don't take any off the top. (*To* HARLAN) I have an idea I'd like to start my own business.

HARLAN: Splendid. Shows an imaginative spirit.

HOMER (*To* MISS CUDDLE): Could you pep it up a bit,

101

sister? (*To* HARLAN) I was thinking of the frozen whale meat business. Do you know that one whale . . . *one whale* . . . can produce several hundred whale steaks . . . not to mention short ribs and whale butts.

HARLAN: I don't see how you can miss!

TONY (*To* HOMER): You want it wet or dry?

HOMER: Leave it the way it is. (TONY *nods. Combs* HOMER's *hair quickly.*)

HARLAN: Will fifty thousand be enough to start?

HOMER: It's better than nothing.

HARLAN: Good. Just sign here. (*Gives* HOMER *a paper and pen.* HOMER *signs.*) Thank you. Take it to the teller and get your money, less a slight interest charge. You also get a free statue of Benjamin Franklin *and* a color TV *plus* a ten transistor radio and, of course, thousands of Green Stamps, candy apples, balloons, blotters and six free rides on the Thunderbolt at Riverside Park next summer.

HOMER (*Takes the paper and starts out*): Thank you. You're the kind of banker America *needs:* a man with a heart. (*He goes out.*)

HARLAN (*To* TONY *and* MISS CUDDLE, *who are now doing a number together*): Knock it off, kids. And send in the chief bookkeeper with ten thousand dollars in pennies. (*He looks at some papers and frowns.* MISS CUDDLE *and* TONY *dance out, a little worried.* HARLAN *looks over papers again, angrily, then gets up and paces about. Sits down, speaks into intercom.*) Send up Slugger Jones, the special officer. (BILL, *the bookkeeper, enters, painfully dragging a heavy bag of ten thousand dollars in pennies.*)

BILL (*Pale and shaking*): You sent for me, O supreme majesty and most merciful ruler of the Fifth National Bank and all its branches and dominions?

HARLAN: Bill, it's time you learned the value of money. I kept you here three nights with only bread and water, hoping you would find that six-cent deficit you showed. This is serious, Bill. It's only six cents but it could just as easily be *six billion dollars.*

BILL: I'll pay it out of my own pocket. I'll do anything . . . *anything.*

HARLAN: You will stay here and go through every single penny, setting aside all the Lincoln heads marked D and minted in 1907. You will select those in which Lincoln's beard has not yet fully grown and where he is wearing sun-glasses.

BILL: But that will take forever.

HARLAN: Bill, I'm fond of you. I've been a father and a mother to you. I've raised your salary in the last nine years all the way up to fifty-eight dollars a week, and you have only one wife and six children to support . . . small children, at that. But Bill, you *must* learn the value of money.

BILL (*Suddenly stiffening*): I've had enough.

HARLAN (*Startled*): What's that? Rebellion?

BILL: I noticed in figuring out one of your loans one day that the interest on ten thousand dollars comes to about thirty thousand dollars . . . and that in the case of small loans it's about one hundred sixty-two percent a year.

HARLAN (*Shrugging*): That's banking! I consider high interest rates the very foundation of capitalism. There is something splendid about one hundred sixty-two percent. (*Special officer* SLUGGER *comes in. He is very tough.*) Ah, Slugger, just in time. We have before us a rebel . . . a man who does not believe in free enterprise. Throw him out!

BILL (*Shoulders braced*): I go bravely. (SLUGGER *grabs* BILL.)

SLUGGER: O.K., boss. What do you want me to do with him?

HARLAN: Out the window. (SLUGGER *pushes* BILL *toward back.*) No, no, not that way. Use one of the windows out in the hall. (SLUGGER *pushes* BILL *out, comes back a moment later, brushing off his hands.*) Did he get hurt?

SLUGGER: How do I know? He hasn't landed yet.

THE END

WHO KILLED DOC ROBIN?

There are many admirers of the two different types of detective heroes. Lately the hardboiled "active" kind seems to be more popular, but for those who remember the good old days, the quiet thoughtful type still has its appeal. The important thing to remember is "cherchez la femme," which translated freely (and like most free translations, it's all wrong!) means "crime does not pay."

❖ ❖ ❖ ❖ ❖

Characters

DOC ROBIN, *a quiet corpse*

TESSIE, *his wife, a suspect*

MRS. FRISKIN, *Tessie's mother, another suspect*

FIFI, *a French maid, a third suspect (ooh, la, la!)*

GILES, *a British butler (the one who usually is the murderer)*

SHERLOCK JONES, *an old-fashioned detective*

HARBOIL LINK, *a new-fashioned detective*

CHARLIE, *a plain policeman*

AT RISE: *A man is stretched out on the floor. There are a revolver, a small bottle, a rope and a knife beside him. Standing in line, looking at* DOC ROBIN *(for it is he!), are*

GILES, *a butler,* FIFI, *a maid,* TESSIE, *his wife, and* MRS. FRISKIN, *his mother-in-law.*

TESSIE: I *do* wish Sherlock Jones, the great detective, would come. The living room looks so messy with Dr. Robin sprawled out there.

MRS. FRISKIN: My dear daughter, I told you when you married Doc he wasn't a *bit* neat. Would a thoughtful and tidy man do away with himself just after the spring cleaning was done?

FIFI: We are not sure, Madame, he *did* do away with himself, no?

TESSIE: Fifi, you can't believe it was murder!

GILES: That, modom, is for Sherlock Jones or Harboil Link to say, not for the likes of us. (SHERLOCK JONES *comes in, trips over something and then stands up.*)

SHERLOCK: Where is the body?

GILES: You just fell over it, sir.

SHERLOCK: Very observant of you, Giles. You're under suspicion, you know. The butler always is.

FIFI (*Walking center and facing audience, she speaks in an aside.*): The butler did not do it.

TESSIE: Mr. Jones, we have also sent for Harboil Link to help you.

SHERLOCK: Rot! That Johnny-come-lately! (*He walks around the body, picks up everything, looks at each item, smells, feels, etc.*) Ah ha! A revolver . . . a bottle of poison . . . a strong rope . . . *and* a very sharp knife!

GILES: Do you suspect foul play, sir?

SHERLOCK: I go by the facts, Giles. Doc Robin is dead. He has taken poison, hung himself, stabbed himself, and shot himself.

TESSIE: My husband was always very thorough.

SHERLOCK: And you, too, Mrs. Robin, are known to be thorough.

TESSIE: Are you accusing me of . . . ?

SHERLOCK: I accuse no one.

FIFI: If he was killed, what is the explanation for such a mistake?

SHERLOCK: A good question. But we must ask another. Did he kill himself? You will notice Doc Robin was not a tall man. He had to stand on a chair to get his neck in this noose.

MRS. FRISKIN: Footprints! On the lovely chair I gave them for Father's Day!

SHERLOCK: Yet he was able, at the same time, to direct a bullet through his back. Meanwhile he was stabbing himself in the stomach, and taking poison.

FIFI: He wished to make sure, eh?

SHERLOCK: Possibly. On the other hand do you notice the red clay on the floor near him? This red clay is found in only one area around here. The Wayward Dog Kennels!

GILES: You think a dog did it?

MRS. FRISKIN: But he loved dogs.

SHERLOCK: Ah, but did dogs love him? *I* know he loved dogs, *he* knew he loved dogs. But did the *dogs* know he loved dogs? (HARBOIL LINK *breezes in. He smiles at everybody, stares at the body thoughtfully, looks around and nods.*)

HARBOIL: I'm Harboil Link. Mrs. Robin sent for me. (*To* SHERLOCK) Still trying to solve crimes with your old-fashioned methods?

SHERLOCK: Perhaps your newer methods can do better?

HARBOIL: Certainly. It is obvious Mrs. Robin has been doing spring cleaning. Every husband hates spring cleaning. Who can listen to the noise of that vacuum cleaner? (*He makes a noise like a vacuum cleaner, runs around aimlessly.*) Mrs. Robin was worse than most. She did her spring cleaning every few weeks. You can tell she has just done it by the fact that the furniture has been moved. See the marks? (*He walks around grunting, pretending to move furniture, deciding on one place and then another.*) Thus we re-enact the crime. Doc Robin came home from a hard day taking out tonsils. He flopped down in his easy chair. But it wasn't there. (*Illustrates*) He jumped up. He was angry. He was psychologically motivated by deep inferior feelings left from the time when he was nine months old and his mother thoughtlessly let a clerk in a department store wrap him up as a twenty-five-pound tub of lard. He called to his wife. (*Calls*) W-i-i-f-f-e! She came. He accused her of moving his chair. She said, "You cad!" He said, "I wish I had married Elsie Furthingale, the baseball cover stitcher!" Mrs. Robin shrieked. (*He shrieks.*) Doc slapped her across the mouth. She accused him of hanging around the soda fountain playing canasta instead of coming home and taking care of her pet guppies.

MRS. FRISKIN: I gave her the two dear guppies. Now there are three hundred. They make friends quickly.

HARBOIL: Yes. A struggle ensued. (*He struggles with himself, alternately shrieking, female style, and howling, male style.*) He threatened to shoot himself. She said, "Go ahead." He did. He missed. He threatened to hang himself. It didn't come out so well. His wife offered him a bottle of poison. He drank it. Nothing happened. It was stale poison. It had been in the house too long. Should have been refrigerated. As a last resort, she handed him a letter opener. No go. Too dull. He had forgotten to sharpen it when he had his skates sharpened. There you are.

SHERLOCK: But then who killed him?

HARBOIL: I have no idea. Are you sure he's *dead?*

GILES: He had better be, sir. They are planning to bury him Wednesday. (CHARLIE, *a policeman, comes in.*)

CHARLIE: What's going on here? I heard a lot of yelling and . . . ah, Sherlock Jones, the great detective . . . and Harboil Link, the other great detective.

SHERLOCK: Who are you?

CHARLIE: I'm Charlie, the dumb cop who always has stupid ideas about the murderer. I'm the guy they always laugh at. Ha,ha,ha,ha! (*He looks around at everybody and then at the body*) This man has been murdered. (*Sniffs around*) He's been killed. (*Examines the floor*) The bottle, rope, knife, and so on, are all plants. Stuff to throw you off the trail. (*He goes over to* GILES.) Butler!

GILES: Yes, sir?

CHARLIE: I notice an odd scar on your neck. This is the sort of scar left by the Poooooowwww Indians in their South American jungle initiation rites.

GILES: It did happen that I served Sir Chester Flugle in South America some years ago.

CHARLIE: Right. There, among the pygmies, you learned of Zinga-Zinga, the root of the wild-eyed Goona-Goona plant, from which a poison is made, so strong . . . that even smelling it for ten minutes may kill a man. (*Sniffs. The others sniff, puzzled.*)

GILES: N-n-nonsense!

CHARLIE: No. Last Tuesday you argued with Doc Robin. You liked the Yankees, he liked the Baltimore Orioles

TESSIE: He was always fond of birds.

109

CHARLIE: Doc called you a name no man can hear himself called without fighting. He called you . . . a . . . a . . . a . . . an egghead! (*They all gasp.*) Later you came back in the middle of a double-header with an ounce of precious Zinga-Zinga. (*He grabs at* GILES' *pocket and removes a box. He takes off the lid. Everybody sniffs and makes horrible faces.*)

GILES: Don't!

CHARLIE: The deadliest poison in the world. A few sniffs . . . a few . . . a . . . a. . . . (*He collapses*).

SHERLOCK: We . . . we . . . must. . . . (*He collapses.* GILES *goes to get the box but falls down.* HARBOIL *and* MRS. FRISKIN *fall on top of him.* FIFI *starts out, but reels and slumps into a chair.*)

TESSIE (*Picks up box and stares at it*): Luckily I was vaccinated against Zinga-Zinga. But whatever am I to do with all these bodies lying around? So terribly untidy! (*Goes to phone, dials*) Hello, Macy's Housekeeping Service? I understand you have a complete cleaning service. Will you come to my house? Yes. Clean the rugs . . . walls . . . linoleum. . . . Wax the floors. . . . Clean upholstered furniture . . . (*Pause*) How about removing dead bodies? Fine. Rightee! I'll expect your men at noon tomorrow. (*Hangs up, looks thoughtfully at bodies*) Oh, dear, I have to get someone to go with me to the Marshalls' wedding reception tonight. (*Goes to phone and dials*) Hello, Marcia . . . something's come up. Doc won't be able to go tonight. He's terribly indisposed.

THE END

ANOTHER CINDERELLA

This is a modern story of Cinderella. The old story of Cinderella never grows old, but it does grow monotonous. The scene is Cinderella's shabby home. As in most of these skits, you don't need to have a shabby home. You can just pretend.

❖ ❖ ❖ ❖ ❖

Characters

CINDERELLA
TOM, *a nice lad; honest, which is all right; poor, which isn't*
THE STEPMOTHER
LOLA ⎫
SOPHIE ⎭ *dopey-looking stepsisters*
THE FAIRY GODMOTHER

AT RISE: CINDERELLA *is sweeping. She talks to herself because there's no one else there at the moment.*

CINDERELLA: Oh, what a life I lead! Woe is me! Cleaning, sweeping, washing dishes, being pushed around by my horrid stepmother. (*She stops sweeping and smiles dreamily.*) But some day . . . *some* day a prince will come for me on a white horse. My wicked stepmother will certainly be surprised . . . especially to see a white horse in the parlor. (*She puts her hand to her ear.*) Hark! (TOM *enters.*)
TOM: Cinderella! Please marry me.

111

CINDERELLA (*Shaking her head*): No. I'm waiting for the Prince to ask me. I had a dream.

TOM: The Prince will never marry you. You'll never even get to meet him. Besides—forgive me, my love—your feet are too big. (*He speaks gently.*) I like big feet, but—

CINDERELLA: I like you, Tom, but we are both poor and we would starve. This wicked country of Poorvania doesn't even have Social Security. The rich have all the money.

TOM: They usually do. (*Pauses thoughtfully*) Some day I, Tom Wiffen, will change all that. I have friends.

CINDERELLA: Please go, Tom. My wicked stepmother is coming. (TOM *goes out.* CINDERELLA *speaks to herself.*) A nice boy, Tom, but no future. (STEPMOTHER *comes in.*)

STEPMOTHER: Cinderella, you look a mess as usual. Even if you combed your hair and had some new clothes, I don't think it would improve you any, though. Now don't stand there dreaming about the Prince. You're not going to the ball. You'd shame us. Your two sisters, Lola and Sophie, *are* going and you know what beauties *they* are. Now get to work . . . clean the fireplace . . . wax the floors . . . paper the walls . . . plough the garden . . . . repair the roof. (*She goes over to* CINDERELLA *and kicks her.*) That's for nothing. That's to demonstrate how wicked I am. (*Laughs fiendishly.*)

CINDERELLA (*Aside*): Could anything worse happen to me?

STEPMOTHER: I could do it again. (LOLA *and* SOPHIE *come in. They are all dressed up. They whirl around showing off and stare at themselves in a mirror.*)

LOLA: I'm so beautiful it makes me dizzy.

CINDERELLA: You were dizzy to start with.

STEPMOTHER (*To* CINDERELLA): What did you say?

CINDERELLA: I said I'm so busy I don't know what to start with.

SOPHIE: How can I be so gorgeous and so smart, too?

CINDERELLA: All you need is a big head, that's all.

STEPMOTHER (*Threatening* CINDERELLA): What was that?

CINDERELLA: I said, it's agreed you're ahead, by all.

SOPHIE (*Comes smiling to* CINDERELLA *and kicks her shin*): That's for nothing, dear stepsister.

LOLA (*Does the same*): We just don't want you to forget how mean we are.

STEPMOTHER (*Beaming*): They're not hypocrites, I'll say that.

LOLA: No. We're honest. (*She dances around clumsily.*) Imagine me dancing with the Prince in the castle at the great ball . . . *me* . . . in *his* arms . . . while Lester Lanin plays, too fast, as usual. The Prince is whirling me around . . . whirling and whirling. Everyone stops to watch us while (*To* CINDERELLA) *you* stay home and beat rugs.

SOPHIE: Imagine me in the Prince's arms . . . he is asking me to marry him . . . I run coyly away . . . (*She pantomimes this*) he chases me. (*This, too.*) . . . I stop . . . he catches me . . . he tries to put his arms around me . . . I elude him . . . I run away . . . (*She pantomimes, but trips over her feet and falls.*)

CINDERELLA: And you fall down a well.

STEPMOTHER: What did you say?

CINDERELLA (*Demurely*): I said, isn't that gown swell.

STEPMOTHER: Hurry now, my dear children, we must go. I'm sure we'll be the hit of the ball and one of you will snag . . . er . . . trap . . . I mean . . . capture the heart of the Prince.

SOPHIE: How can we miss?

LOLA: You either have it or, like Cinderella, you don't have it. (*They go out laughing gaily and taking a poke at* CINDERELLA *to show their feelings about her.*)

CINDERELLA (*Sadly*): That's the way it always is with me. "Don't call us, we'll call you." I am so young and hopeful . . . and nothing ever happens . . . nothing but housemaid's knee. I'm too young to die—of housemaid's knee, anyway. (*She dances around the room, pretending she is talking to the Prince.*) Oh, thank you, Prince Charming. That's an odd name. Prince Charming. Most Princes are Rudolph or Philip or Otto. . . . What? A diamond necklace worth seven million . . . and you got it wholesale, at that? Oh, it's dazzling. But I couldn't. No, not from a stranger. Not on such short acquaintance. . . . See me next Tuesday? . . . Dance? I'd love to, but dear Princey, we've danced eleven consecutive dances. Won't this start a palace revolution? . . . Very well, I am yours to command. (*She dances around with "him."*) *While this is going on, the* FAIRY GODMOTHER *has tiptoed in. If possible, the* FAIRY GODMOTHER *should be oddly dressed. She certainly should have a stick with a star on the end. This you got to have.*)

FAIRY GODMOTHER (*As* CINDERELLA *sees her, and stops dancing*): What are you, some kind of kook?

CINDERELLA: Oh! Who are you?

FAIRY GODMOTHER: Your fairy godmother. Who else? I have come to transform your life with spells and incantations. Do you have a pumpkin and some mice around?

CINDERELLA: Gee, I'm sorry. We don't.

FAIRY GODMOTHER: That's how it goes. The one time you *need* a pumpkin and some mice, you can't find them. If you didn't *need* them. . . . (*She shrugs.*) All right. Go into the other room and wait patiently. I will perform

114

magic spells and work myself into quite a tizzy. My heart is really in this one. (CINDERELLA *goes out. The* FAIRY GODMOTHER *jumps up and down, wails, waves her wand around and then goes to a window upstage and looks out.*) So who needs a coach and horses? I knew I should have gone into spring training. (*She jumps up and down and wails and moans again, then stops and looks out of window.*) Nothing yet. I don't know how I ever got my Fairy Godmother's diploma. Even now I can't practice in France or Canada. (*She starts chanting.*)

> Oh, ye spirits and ye forces,
> Get ye up a coach and horses!
> Get up a lovely lamé gown,
> So this poor kid can go to town!
> Make it snappy.
> Make it happy.
> Hey! Yeah!

(*She dances around grotesquely, possibly repeating the chant until* CINDERELLA *comes back.* CINDERELLA *is wearing a nice dress, and green shoes. Her hair is neatly done, and she has make-up on.*) Cinderella! I wouldn't recognize you.

CINDERELLA: I feel so wonderful.

FAIRY GODMOTHER (*At window*): Well, I couldn't work up a coach and horses and footmen. But I did manage a chauffeur and a sports convertible. Not new, but used by only one owner—a little old lady who drove in the five-hundred-mile Indianapolis Sweepstakes.

CINDERELLA (*Looking out window*): Oh, it's beautiful! And the chauffeur is so handsome.

FAIRY GODMOTHER: Yes. But stick to the script. You can't fall in love with the chauffeur. At midnight, that car turns into a Hubbard squash, and the chauffeur turns into a mushroom—a handsome mushroom, but a mushroom. (*She looks down at* CINDERELLA's *feet, shakes her head.*) I don't know if this is going to work. You must wear size nine shoes.

CINDERELLA: I do.

FAIRY GODMOTHER: Well, a glass slipper is a glass slipper. Actually, that is a poor translation from the French. It was really a *green* slipper. A glass slipper is nonsense. You do the Twist in glass slippers and you shatter your shoes to pieces. Now, get going. Remember, midnight and you've had it. Meanwhile, it'll be a ball.

CURTAIN
* * * *

A curtain can fall (as we say above), or the lights can go out, or, barring that, a capable lad can announce, "That's the end of the first scene. Two hours elapse before the next scene, so synchronize your watches." Then we have Scene Two. The setting is the same as Scene One. At rise, the STEPMOTHER, SOPHIE, *and* LOLA *come in wearily.*

STEPMOTHER: Well, how did I know there was going to be a revolution?

LOLA: The Prince still had two hours to dance with us. But he kept dancing with that little thing in the green slippers.

SOPHIE: Did those slippers look like green bottle glass to you?

LOLA: No. (*Pause*) I think the Prince is a fink, anyway.

SOPHIE: Really very homely when you get close to him.

STEPMOTHER: Who got close to him? (*Pause*) Where's Cinderella. (*Calls*) Cinderella! (*Pause*) That girl has got to go.

116

SOPHIE: Get her down here. I feel like kicking somebody.

LOLA: Well, at least the revolution showed the Prince *he* wasn't so much.

SOPHIE: That'll teach him to ignore us.

STEPMOTHER (*Calls*): Cinderella! It's after midnight . . . where are you? (*The old* CINDERELLA *comes in. She looks the same, but she has a sparkle about her.*)

CINDERELLA: Here I am. I was watching the late news.

STEPMOTHER: You be here when we need you. Get my bathrobe and make me some tea.

CINDERELLA: Make it yourself, you old witch.

LOLA: What? You heard Mama. Do what you're told, or you will be put out into the night to starve.

CINDERELLA: Like mother, like daughter. You and your big mouth.

LOLA: What's come over you? Do what you're told. (*She takes a poke at* CINDERELLA, *but it doesn't work.* CINDERELLA *grabs her and tosses her aside.*)

SOPHIE (*To* STEPMOTHER): I told you not to let her watch wrestling on television! (*The* STEPMOTHER *makes like a wrestler, crouching and creeping up on* CINDERELLA. *The sisters do the same. They are about to pounce on* CINDERELLA *when* TOM *comes in, holding a green slipper.* TOM *should be wearing a fancy uniform or a gold crown or something to show authority.*)

TOM: Stop this! I command it. (*They all straighten up.*) I swore when I overthrew the Prince because of his wicked ways that I would marry the beautiful girl who left her green slipper at the ball. I want you all to try it on, and if it fits the wicked stepmother—I'll have to think of something else. (*He puts the slipper down. The* STEPMOTHER *grunts and groans, but she can't walk in the slipper.*) Your feet are too small. (SOPHIE *tries, but she can't keep the slipper on, either.*) You swim in it. (LOLA *tries, with the same result.*) Small feet, small brain.

CINDERELLA (*Shyly*): May I try?

TOM: Certainly. (*He puts the slipper on her foot. She takes the other slipper from her pocket and puts it on.*) A perfect fit! I thought I'd never find anyone with feet like this. I am pledged to marry you, Cinderella. You will be my princess of Poorvania. Of course, I'm changing the name of the kingdom to Paradise Acres. (*He holds out his arms.*) Cinderella, I love you. Big feet and all.

STEPMOTHER (*Hugging* CINDERELLA): I knew you'd make it, dear.

TOM (*Pulling* CINDERELLA *away*): Would you like me to hang your stepmother and stepsisters, dear? It would be sort of fun.

CINDERELLA: No, Prince Tom. My heart is so full of joy, I would not hang them. Let them live in the castle with us where I can kick them around at my pleasure.

TOM: You're a *good* kid. (*Pause*) Come! Let us prepare for the wedding! (FAIRY GODMOTHER *has come prancing in.*)

FAIRY GODMOTHER: Congratulations. I knew I would work it out somehow. (*Pause*) My fee, please. It's $50, according to the minimum wage of The Fairy Godmothers' and Witches' Union, Local 117, American Federation of Magic. (TOM *hands her the money.*)

STEPMOTHER (*To* FAIRY GODMOTHER): You've done such a good job—here are two new customers—lovely girls you can work with right now. (*She grabs* LOLA *and* SOPHIE, *who wail as she pushes them up to the* FAIRY GOD-MOTHER. *Curtain.*)

THE END

GRADUATION ADDRESS

Most books and speeches—especially speeches—could be shortened with no loss to reader or listener. But if everything were reduced to proper proportions, there would be few books published (after all, who'd want to pay five dollars for a one-page book!), and most speeches would be over before the audience is comfortably seated.

❖ ❖ ❖ ❖ ❖

Characters
BIFF, *who has to give a speech*
ELSIE ⎫
TOM ⎪
DIANE ⎬ *fellow students*
WALDO ⎭

AT RISE: BIFF *is holding a typewritten manuscript in his hand. The others stand around him.*

BIFF: I start this graduation address off with, "Dr. Clune, distinguished guests, teachers and fellow students. . . ."
ELSIE: It's great so far.
BIFF: I want to keep it simple and yet impressive. You don't graduate from Chutney High School *every* day, you know.
DIANE: You're lucky if you *ever* do it.
WALDO: I was at the bottom of the class all year.
TOM: Well, they teach the same thing at both ends.

BIFF: Look, this is a great event in my life. I wish you'd help me. Now, I go on. . . . "I stand here proudly to address you. We, the graduating class of old Chutney, are going forth, bearing the torch of learning onward and upward, ever and ever forward! We are the coming generation, and before us lies the future. . . ."

ELSIE: It's thrilling . . . but . . . there's one little thing . . . see if you don't agree . . . you say, "I stand here proudly to address you." It's pretty obvious you're standing there.

TOM: Sure. And naturally you're proud. I mean if you *say* you're proud, some people might think that maybe the rest of us aren't proud.

WALDO: Right. And everyone knows you're there to address people. You're not going to do card tricks.

DIANE: Or sing folk songs.

BIFF: Hmmmnnn. Well . . . maybe.

ELSIE: Another thing . . . everybody *knows* we're the graduating class of old Chutney . . .

TOM: Correct. And I don't like "going forth bearing the torch of learning." People don't bear torches any more, and besides, what is a torch of learning?

DIANE: It's obscure.

BIFF: It was just a literary touch.

WALDO: And what's this with the . . . "onward and upward, ever and ever forward"? Isn't that self-evident?

ELSIE: Sure . . . no one expects we're going backward and downward, ever and ever retreating.

BIFF: Yeah. Maybe there's something in that. Well . . . we'll strike some things out. (*He crosses out with pencil five or six lines on the manuscript.*) Let's go on. (*Reads*) "On us weighs the burden . . ."

DIANE: Hold it! That part . . . "We are the coming generation, and before us lies the future." Naturally, we're the coming generation. You fellows don't even shave yet. And where else can the future lie if not before us?

BIFF (*A little annoyed as he crosses lines out*): O.K. O.K. (*Reads*) "On us weighs the burden of shaping the world closer to the heart's desire. We, and we alone, must do the task of putting our shoulders to the wheel and rowing bravely upstream until the glorious mountain peak of happiness and security is reached . . ."

ELSIE: Whoa! Whoa! "On us weighs the burden"? I don't feel anything.

TOM: What he means is we have a job to do.

DIANE: O.K. But how about "shaping the world closer to the heart's desire"? What does that mean? Should we make it square?

WALDO: Yeah. It sounds as if we were going to squeeze it into a football.

BIFF: I'll cross it out, I guess. I was just being poetic. (*Crosses out*) I'll go on. There isn't much more. As I look ahead, I see quite a bit I can cut out.

ELSIE: We'd better stay with what we have so far. "We, and we alone, must do the task of putting our shoulders to the wheel and rowing bravely upstream. . . ."

TOM: Why can't we row *down*stream?

BIFF: Well . . . I guess . . . it's just a choice of words.

TOM: Good. But what are we trying to do? Reach the mountain peak of success. . . .

BIFF (*Correcting him quickly*): Happiness.

TOM: O.K. But by rowing upstream?

DIANE: With our noses to the ground and our ears to the grindstone?

BIFF (*Annoyed*): I didn't say anything about that. (*He is now busy striking out paragraph after paragraph.*)

WALDO: People don't really put their shoulders to the wheel any more. They have automatic transmissions.

ELSIE: Besides, it's a mixed metaphor. You can't row the boat and put your shoulder to the wheel at the same time.

BIFF: All right. All right!

DIANE: Why does happiness have to be on top of a mountain?

BIFF: Forget it. (*He keeps striking out stuff.*)

ELSIE: Why not just say: "We have a job to do and we'll do it"? That's nice and vague.

TOM: *Too* vague. How about: "We, the cavalry of tomorrow, shall charge across the bloody corpses of poverty, ignorance, and prejudice until we slaughter the defenders of evil and graft!"

DIANE: It's ghastly. Cavalry? Horses? Where will we get the horses?

WALDO: Nobody fights with cavalry or on battlefields anymore. (*To* BIFF) How're you doing?

BIFF (*Bitterly*): This is what I have left: "Dr. Clune, distinguished guests, teachers and fellow students . . . *I thank you.*"

WALDO: That's wonderful!

ELSIE: That's just right.

DIANE: Read it again.

BIFF (*Reading*): "Dr. Clune, distinguished guests, teachers and fellow students . . . I thank you." (*All cheer wildly and clap* BIFF *on the back.*)

THE END

CAN'T GET THERE
FROM HERE, MEBBE

This is a brief skit, often called a blackout because it helps to have the room go suddenly dark as the last line is spoken. (Someone can stand at the light switch and turn off the lights at the end if you want to try this as a blackout.) The setting is a general store in Punkus, Vermont, or Deadbeat, Oklahoma. All that is needed is a sign saying: GENERAL STORE—POST OFFICE—COURT HOUSE AND SHOE REPAIRS. *A cracker barrel and a rocking chair would help.*

❖ ❖ ❖ ❖ ❖

Characters

DEWEY FUSS, *proprietor of a general store*
TIM ⎱ *a young married couple who*
MARY ⎰ *are out driving*

AT RISE: DEWEY FUSS *is rocking in a chair. He wears red suspenders, a blue work shirt, and jeans. The telephone rings, and* DEWEY *answers it.*

DEWEY: Hello, Dewey Fuss, General Store, Postmaster, shoe repairs and fines levied for speedin'. . . . What, Sarah? No, I don't have any artichokes for your husband. Haven't had any since 1946. Gettin' to be quite the dude, your husband. (*Hangs up*) Consarned invention, always ringin' . . . and when it does . . . always somebody at the other end jabbering. (*Goes back to rocking chair*) Be glad when Coolidge runs again. (TIM *and* MARY *come in.*)

TIM: Hello.

MARY: Hello.

DEWEY: How be ye, strangers? Welcome to Vermont. Leave her the way you found her. Fine place to live. Good stock.

TIM (*Looking around store*): *You* don't have much stock in this store, do you?

DEWEY: Nope.

MARY (*Looking around*): Hardly anything.

DEWEY: Yep.

TIM: Why is that?

DEWEY: Used to have a lot of stock. Kept me busy sellin' it. Never had any chance to *reee*-lax. So I cut out most of the stuff. Don't hardly make a sale now.

MARY: How can you make money that way?

DEWEY: Low overhead.

TIM: Well, we won't bother you for long. Can you tell us the way to Bennington?

DEWEY: Nope.

MARY: Maybe you know the road to Granville, New York?

DEWEY: Nope.

TIM: Are we on Route 62-C?

DEWEY: Don't know.

MARY: Are we far from the junction with 78-B?

DEWEY: Not knowin', can't say.

TIM (*Getting weary*): Does the road to Hudson Falls run in back of your place here?

DEWEY: Don't know. Never looked.

MARY (*A bit annoyed*): We're nearly out of gas. Is there a filling station nearby?

DEWEY: Don't know.

TIM: Well, is there any place in town we could stay for the night?

DEWEY: Not knowin', can't say.

MARY: How far is it from here to the New York state line?

DEWEY: Can't rightly say.

TIM: Are we anywhere *near* the Massachusetts Turnpike?

DEWEY: Don't know.

TIM (*Angrily*): You don't know *much,* do you?

DEWEY (*Calmly*): Nope. (*Pause*) But I'm not lost.

THE END

LOVE SEEKS A WAY

This is the story of true love that didn't run smooth and an automobile that didn't run any too well, either. It requires considerable pantomime. The scene is outside an automobile salesroom.

❖ ❖ ❖ ❖ ❖

Characters
SNAPPY, *a quick-witted automobile salesman*
HAPPY, *his partner*
MAY, *a young girl who wants to get married*
JOHN, *a young man who is ready*

AT RISE: JOHN *and* MAY, *about seventeen years old, pretend to be looking in a window from the street.*

MAY: Isn't that a beautiful automobile! (JOHN *pretends to look in window.*)

JOHN: That's a real cool job.

MAY: It says, "The Razzle Six—America's Finest Economy Car. NEW. $500."

JOHN: I can't believe it.

MAY (*Looking soulfully at* JOHN): That would do the trick.

JOHN: What would?

MAY: Our parents say we're too young and irresponsible

126

to get married. If we had a car that would *prove* we were mature and everything.

JOHN: That's right. When you have your own car you're grown-up. (*Pause*) But where would we live?

MAY: In the car. It probably has a heater and a radio. I could fry eggs with the cigarette-lighter . . .

JOHN: But five hundred dollars . . . ?

MAY: We could get it from the bank.

JOHN: I was in the bank yesterday. They wouldn't even give me a calendar.

MAY (*Looking in window again*): It says "Only Ten Dollars Down."

JOHN: I know. And then fifty dollars a month. I only get a dollar a week for allowance.

MAY: I get a dollar a week, too, for baby-sitting.

JOHN: I don't want you working after we're married.

MAY: Let's go in and look at it, anyway. (*They pretend to open a door and walk a few steps, stopping finally and staring at a couple of chairs and a wheel or something to represent the Razzle Six.*) Ooooh. Isn't it beautiful? (*Pause*) Oh, John, I love you with all my heart, and I'll love you forever and ever. . . . We just *have* to get this car to prove we're adults.

JOHN: It sure is a beauty. (*Turns and smiles at* MAY) I love you, too, dear. I will never say an angry word to you, or argue with you or be unkind or anything after we're married.

MAY: If our parents only knew how much we love each other and how grown-up we are! If they only knew that I will always love you and let you be the boss and never nag or pick on you or. . . . (*Pause*) I certainly will be a lot better for you than that blonde Jones girl you went around with.

JOHN: That was six months ago. I was just a kid. *I'll* certainly never be like that old man of twenty-four you were so crazy about . . . Bill Stiffen.

MAY: That was last summer. I was a baby. My parents liked him because he was making $15,000 a year. They said he could support me.

JOHN: So could I, if I were making $15,000 a year. (*Two salesmen come out, rubbing their hands. One is* SNAPPY *and the other is* HAPPY. *They smile and bow in an overly polite manner.*)

SNAPPY: I'm Snappy.

HAPPY: I'm Happy. We're here to serve you day and night.

SNAPPY: Your wants are our wants. Your needs are our needs.

HAPPY: Your happiness is our happiness.

SNAPPY: We sell Razzle automobiles. We gladly finance any sale. Our rates are as low as 3 per cent.

JOHN: Say! That would only be fifteen dollars a year on the $500 model.

HAPPY: Not exactly. There are insurance, legal fees, closing fees, opening fees . . .

SNAPPY (*Taking out pencil and paper and figuring*): State and federal taxes, city taxes, county taxes, town taxes, excise taxes and sales taxes.

MAY (*Going over to car*): Is this the $500 model?

HAPPY: Yes. The lowest priced, cheapest, most compact economy car in the world.

SNAPPY (*To* JOHN): It comes to about $300 extra for financing and taxes. How much do you make a week?

JOHN: I'm still in school. I get a dollar a week allowance.

SNAPPY (*Not a bit perturbed*): I see. Of course we allow you up to ten years to pay . . . (*Figures again while* MAY *is pretending to look at the car with* HAPPY) You'd have to get your allowance up to three dollars a week. Could you sell homemade lemonade in front of your house . . . things like that?

JOHN: Sure. Of course I'd have to support a wife, too.

SNAPPY: Well, then, you'd just have to sell *more* lemonade. . . . Let's look at this beautiful job. (SNAPPY *and* JOHN *join* MAY *and* HAPPY *and pretend to look at the car.*)

HAPPY (*To* SNAPPY): These two are about to be joined in blessed wedlock.

SNAPPY: Ah, marriage! The very swimming pool of bliss. How lucky you are to have found each other! How fortunate you are to be starting on the joyful road to Paradise in a Razzle Six.

MAY: Could we take it out and drive it?

HAPPY: It's the only model we have.

JOHN: Maybe we could drive it in here?

SNAPPY: It's not ready. (*Pause*) Look at those beautiful tires. (JOHN *pretends to kick one. He backs away nervously.*)

HAPPY: You kick awfully hard. You kicked the wheel off. (*He bends down, pantomimes picking up the wheel and pushing it back on.*)

SNAPPY: Makes tire changes possible in a jiffy.

MAY: Look at the lovely, shining bumper! (*She puts a foot on it as if attempting to stand. She jumps back quickly, nearly losing her balance.* SNAPPY *sighs, pretends to lift up bumper and set it back in place.*)

HAPPY: Notice the rugged fenders.

JOHN: Say! (*He grasps what would be the fender with both hands, falls back as if he had it in his arms. He looks down at his arms.*) I guess I pulled too hard. (*Pretends to hand fender to* SNAPPY, *who puts it back.*)

SNAPPY: Makes fender dents easy to fix. You just knock off

the fender, take it home and hammer it back into shape with a teaspoon.

MAY: Let's look in the trunk. We'll need space on our honeymoon. (*She edges up to* JOHN *and he hugs her.*) Niagara Falls—I've always dreamed of it!

JOHN: I thought I decided on Atlantic City.

MAY: Well . . . we won't argue . . . (*She pretends to open the trunk. Peering, a little disappointed*) Is this the trunk?

HAPPY: Yes. We had to decide between leg room and trunk room, and we decided people are more worried about their legs than their trunks. Ha ha. It's just a token trunk. Room for a couple of books and two or three sandwiches. The $3,000 model has a nice trunk, large enough for your mother-in-law.

JOHN: This is a six cylinder car, isn't it?

SNAPPY: Not exactly. The Razzle Six is a four. The Razzle Twelve is a six and the de luxe 250 horsepower Razzle Twin Six is a 150 horsepower eight. It sounds a little confusing but *we* understand it.

MAY: It sounds mixed up.

HAPPY: Not at all. People want economy *and* power. We call it a 250 horsepower Twin Six but it actually costs the same to operate as a 150 horsepower eight. You save a hundred horsepower and four cylinders, and we charge you not a cent extra. (*All these people may have little pamphlets to look at for reference so they can read them instead of memorizing these lines.*)

MAY: Can we sit in it?

SNAPPY: Certainly. We had real bucket seats at first—real, old oaken buckets—but people got stuck in them. You realize this is a really *compact* compact. (MAY *tries to*

open door, tugs a little and then holds up her hand to
SNAPPY.)

MAY: The handle came off.

SNAPPY: Another interesting feature in case you want to take them in the house and polish them. (JOHN *pretends to reach in and pull open the door. He jumps gingerly and backs away as if the door has come off.*)

MAY: Ooooh. The door came right off, too.

HAPPY: This is a convertible, you know. In hot weather you can get a nice breeze by just knocking off the doors. (*Pause*) Step in. (MAY *and* JOHN *both go for the driver's seat.*)

MAY: *I* like to drive.

JOHN: I'll be the head of the family.

MAY: I know, but I'll need the car to take the kids to school and go shopping and all.

JOHN: I don't quite see it that way.

MAY: Don't be selfish. Don't take the car down to the office and just *park* it all day.

JOHN: All right. All right. (*He gets in and squats down in a very uncomfortable position, banging his head on the roof twice.* MAY *squats down, head bent, and pretends to take the wheel.* JOHN *glares at* MAY. *She turns up her nose at him. She tries the wheel. It comes off.*)

MAY: The steering wheel came off!

JOHN: Women drivers!

HAPPY: Put it back on. We like a lot of play in the wheel. (MAY *puts it back. She pretends to turn key and give it gas. Car shakes furiously while* HAPPY *and* SNAPPY *dash around pretending to push doors back on, prop up fenders, etc.* MAY *and* JOHN *jiggle and jounce and sway sideways, really all shook up, as* HAPPY *and* SNAPPY *fi-*

nally pretend to stretch out their arms and hold the car together.)

SNAPPY: Exhilarating ride, no? (MAY *finally stops the car. She and* JOHN *sit there a moment, dazed and shaken. They get out bent and staggering.)*

JOHN: It doesn't feel like a four-cylinder car.

HAPPY: It's really two cylinders working in two cycles. This saves a lot on spark plugs. No extra charge.

MAY: And it's only $500?

SNAPPY: Stripped. You'd want wheels, wouldn't you? They'd be . . . uh . . . $200 extra.

HAPPY: You'd want the motor, I suppose. That's . . . uh . . . optional . . . but it runs an added $400. The doors and windows will cost you $300 more. Tires run about $200. Brakes, gas tank, windshield wipers, exhaust pipe and ashtray mount up to about $600 more. There are a few other options . . . hmnn . . . well . . . make it a round $2500 fully equipped with Kleenex, rabbit's foot, jack and automatically emptying ashtray . . .

SNAPPY: Yes. The ashtray has a hole that leads under the car and the ashes just fall on the road . . .

HAPPY: And a sticker reading: Souvenir of Atlantic City. (*He beams.*)

MAY: We're going to Niagara Falls.

JOHN: Atlantic City.

MAY (*Sharply*): I told everyone Niagara Falls.

JOHN: *You* told everyone? I'm not starting out married life being bossed around. (*He kicks the car angrily.* HAPPY *dashes to car, pretending to pick up the door again.*)

MAY (*Banging her fist on fender*): I can tell *you*, that I have no intention of being the wife of a man who has to have his *own* way all the time. (SNAPPY *wearily puts fender back.*)

JOHN: *My* own way! Oh, brother! Nag, nag, nag. I can't stand a woman always picking on me. (*He kicks at rear of car.* HAPPY *dashes to put it back in place.*)

MAY: You call *that* nagging? What about the way you're shouting and yelling?

JOHN: Why shouldn't I shout and yell when you're making a scene in public?

MAY: I'm certainly glad I found out your true character *before* we were married. Believe *me,* I can see what happened to the Jones girl.

JOHN: I could tell right away when you wanted to drive that you were the domineering type . . . (*He pushes both hands against the car. Both* HAPPY *and* SNAPPY *rush, trying to shore the whole thing up.*)

MAY: Goodbye. I've never been so insulted. Never try to see me again. If you'd ever given me a ring, I'd throw it right in your face. (*She starts for the door.*)

JOHN: If I had ever given you a ring, I should have had my head examined. My mother *said* you were just leading me on.

MAY: We're *through!* (*She pretends to open door of salesroom. As she walks out she pretends to slam door. It falls off, and* HAPPY *and* SNAPPY *run to put it back in place. When* MAY *is gone,* JOHN *stands there disconsolately. He kicks at the floor a few times, and* HAPPY *and* SNAPPY *dash over and move him hastily out of reach of the car.*)

SNAPPY: Don't be sad. The course of true love never did run smooth.

HAPPY: Cheer up. You're young yet.

SNAPPY: You'll soon find somebody else.

JOHN (*Shaking his head sadly*): No. It's too late. It's too late.

HAPPY: Too late for what?

JOHN: Too late to find another date for tonight! (*He vigorously stamps his foot on the floor several times. At this* SNAPPY *and* HAPPY *look over their shoulders at the car. At the fourth vigorous stomp, they rush simultaneously to put back the fallen fenders, doors, etc. Curtain.*)

THE END

THE SUPERMARKET BLUES

The setting of this skit is the checkout counter in a supermarket. Two rails would suffice, plus a table or something at the right for the checkout girl. Actors can use pantomime to pretend pushing carts, taking groceries out to put on checkout counter, etc. One "must" is a large lettered card about which we shall learn more at the end. The other is a large doll, well-wrapped in a blanket, that is supposed to be a baby.

◇ ◇ ◇ ◇ ◇

Characters

MABEL ROYCE ⎫
GERT PIFFLE ⎪
GEORGE READE ⎬ *customers*
HERBIE GREEN ⎭
MAUDE, *a checkout girl*
MR. POTTER, *manager of the store*

AT RISE: MAUDE *stands at the register, pale and haggard. She should be hatless and wear a colored smock. A number of people (wearing hats and coats to show they are customers) stand in line. First person in line is* MABEL ROYCE, *and behind her is* GERT PIFFLE. MABEL *is putting her cans and bottles on the checkout counter when she notices* GERT.

MABEL: Gert! I haven't seen you since you fell off the platform at the Women's Club supper.

GERT: I never did give my talk on my trip to Bermuda.

MABEL (*Matter-of-factly*): Oh, it didn't matter. We'd all heard it ten times anyway.

GERT: I sprained my ankle. I sued.

MABEL: When does it come up in court? (MAUDE *is shifting back and forth impatiently, biting her nails.*)

GERT: In about three years. The courts are way behind.

MABEL: You could be dead by that time. Who'd get the money in that case?

GERT: My brother-in-law, probably. He gets everything else. Haven't you put on a lot of weight, Mabel? Or is the dress you're wearing a size smaller than usual? (GEORGE READE, *behind the two, shakes his head in annoyance.*)

GEORGE: I think she's just right. Anyway, maybe she didn't get fat. Maybe she got *shorter* and that makes her look fatter. Let's get a move on here. (HERBIE GREEN, *behind* GEORGE, *has a baby in his arms. He chucks it under the chin now and then and ad libs, "Gootchie, gootchie! Oogie . . . googie!"*)

HERBIE: Come on. Let's go. (*To* GEORGE) Don't encourage them. They'll start exchanging diets and we'll be here all night.

MAUDE (*To women*): Please, ladies, you're holding up the checkout line.

MABEL (*To* GERT): You realize I voted for this girl as the most pleasant and agreeable checkout girl of the year in 1963?

GERT: She was new then. She didn't know any better.

MAUDE (*Wearily*): I didn't have corns then, either.

GERT: Corn! That reminds me, I forgot to get corn. Oh, it

136

isn't worth going back for. Besides, I hate to trouble all these people in line.

MABEL: Who are they? Ordinary citizens like you and me. Not as good, maybe. Is it going to hurt them to be a little inconvenienced? Why don't they call up some expensive delicatessen and have their groceries delivered?

HERBIE (*Calling to* MABEL): Let's go, Chubby.

MABEL: Chubby! Don't you dare call me Chubby. (*She tries to hit* HERBIE.)

GEORGE: Don't strike him, madam. He's a mother. I mean —he has a baby in his arms.

MAUDE (*Very nervous now*): Please! I'm responsible for anything that happens at the checkout counter. No fights. If you want to fight, pay your bill and go outside.

GERT (*To* MABEL): The nerve of some people. That's how they are today—rude, thoughtless, thinking only of themselves.

MABEL: I was brought up to be considerate. My mother always said, "Mabel, if we didn't give you anything else, we gave you good manners." And they *didn't* give me anything else.

GEORGE: Oh, my aching back! Will you please hurry? All I have is two yeast cakes.

HERBIE: Why don't you go to the fast checkout?

GEORGE: This *is* the fast checkout.

MABEL (*To* MAUDE): Is this "Great Big Giant Economy" size cheaper than the plain "Giant" size?

MAUDE (*Wearily*): I don't know, ma'am.

GERT: What they do is just use a bigger *box*.

MABEL: You notice they don't *have* any *small* size.

GERT: That's right. The small size is the "Giant" size. The medium size is the "Big Giant" size. The large size is the "Great Big Giant Economy" size.

MABEL (*To* MAUDE): Which is cheaper?

MAUDE (*She looks at box*): I'm so tired I can't see. (*She calls.*) Oh, Mr. Potter!

POTTER (*Entering*): What is it? You know I'm busy, Maude.

HERBIE: *You're* busy? Do *you* have to shop and take care of a baby at the same time?

GEORGE: The manager! All I ever see him do is sample the watermelon.

GERT: I saw him pack once. He puts the eggs on the bottom. On top he drops a cantaloupe. Then some soft tomatoes. On top of this, a hammer and ten pounds of sugar. When I got home, I had a *raw* Spanish omelet.

MABEL: *He's* busy! He's not even married!

MAUDE (*To* POTTER): Which is the cheapest? The "Great Big Giant Economy" size or the "Giant" size?

POTTER: Well, let me see. . . . I'll need my magnifying glass to see the weights . . . hmm . . . four and three-seventeenths ounces at forty cents. . . . This one is nine and four-thirty-seconds ounces at three for two dollars and sixty-nine . . . and eleven and fourteen-sixteenths ounces and eleven milligrams. . . .

MABEL: Milligrams yet!

GERT: Very fattening.

POTTER (*Does calculations for a while, smiles finally*): The "Giant Economy" size is the most expensive. The small, expensive size is the cheapest *provided* you use the coupon for nine cents off on a gallon of fig juice. (*He walks away.*)

GEORGE: Come on, come on . . .

MABEL (*To* MAUDE): I'll have to go back to get the fig juice. (*To* GERT) Don't let anyone take my place. You know how these men are. Pushy. (*She makes her way,*

138

knocking against the men, getting stuck, shoving and so on, until she goes off.)

GEORGE: Look, all I have is two yeast cakes.

HERBIE: My wife is going to have the police looking for me.

GERT (*To* MAUDE): They're no gentlemen.

HERBIE: Tell her a lady would let a man with an innocent baby in his arms go first.

GERT (*To* MAUDE, *who is about to tear her hair*): Tell him a decent mother wouldn't trust her helpless infant to a man roaming around a supermarket.

HERBIE (*To* MAUDE): Tell her I have a wife sick in bed.

GERT: Sick in bed, sure. From what? From taking down storm windows and mowing the lawn while *he* sits on the front porch smoking cigars. (HERBIE *forces his way to* MAUDE. GERT *tries to push him back. He shakes her off. She gets a wrestling hold on him. He struggles and puts baby down on counter.*)

HERBIE: How dare you strike a man with a baby? (GERT *continues to wrestle.* GEORGE *tries to help* HERBIE *and they all get involved.*)

MAUDE (*Holding up the baby and screaming*): Mr. Potter! Yoo-hoo!

POTTER (*Appears, shaking and nervous*): Don't *ever* scream like that. I had seventeen cantaloupes piled up and they all fell down. (MABEL *now appears and tries to wiggle her way to the front between the others.* POTTER, *from a distance, looks at baby and points to it.*) They're on sale today. Young tom turkeys. Seven dollars and a half with the coupon which also entitles you to a quart of fig juice.

MAUDE (*To* POTTER): *What* did you say?

POTTER (*Gesturing vaguely at baby*): I said seven dollars and a half for that. (MAUDE *shakes her head and shrugs.*)

139

MAUDE (*To* HERBIE): Seven dollars and a half.

HERBIE: For what?

MAUDE (*Handing back the baby*): For *this*.

HERBIE: But I had that when I came in. (*Coos at baby*)

POTTER (*Suspiciously*): Where did you get it?

HERBIE: What do you mean?

GERT (*Yelling*): *I* was first in line!

POTTER (*To* HERBIE): There's been a lot of shoplifting here.

HERBIE: Are you calling me a crook?

MABEL (*Pushing through*): It's about time women were shown some respect. (*She puts her groceries on counter.* MAUDE *looks nervously at her watch, hesitates, stares at* MABEL's *groceries, shrugs and then rings up one large sum.*)

MAUDE (*Looking nervously at watch again*): This is only an estimate. Twelve dollars and eleven cents. (MABEL *pays her.* MAUDE *packs groceries and hands bag to* MABEL, *who goes off.* GERT *squirms to the front.* MAUDE *looks behind nervously.* GERT *puts her things on counter as* MAUDE *checks watch and then rings up items.*) Sixteen eighty-two.

GERT: I could buy it for fifteen ninety-one at Chipper's Discount Grocery in Albuquerque. (*She pays.*)

MAUDE: You wouldn't get the free fly-swatter. (*Packs wildly and hands bag to* GERT, *who goes off.* GEORGE *comes up, smiling, breathless, triumphant finally.*)

GEORGE: At last it's my turn. I'm next. Thank goodness!

MAUDE: Sorry! This is the time for my coffee break. Next checkout, please. (*She puts up a large sign:* NEXT COUNTER *with an arrow underneath the words.* GEORGE *screams and collapses. Curtain.*)

THE END

THE LOAFER

This is a domestic comedy and contains a situation that occurs all too often. Not in our families, of course. But in other people's. Our skit takes place in a living room. There should be a couch onstage.

❖ ❖ ❖ ❖ ❖

Characters

GEORGE, *a loafing, sponging brother-in-law. He has a cultivated mind, but it was never fertilized.*

ETHEL, *a long-suffering housewife who has suffered too long*

BILL, *her husband and companion in suffering*

MR. SPIFF, *Bill's boss, the chief engineer of an automobile factory*

AT RISE: GEORGE, *the loafer, is stretched out, lounging on the couch, eating candy or cake, reading a magazine, and yawning now and then.* ETHEL *comes in and stares at him.*

ETHEL: George, don't you ever get sick of loafing?

GEORGE (*Lazily*): No. It suits me fine, thanks.

ETHEL: Well, I get sick of watching you.

GEORGE: I'll go in the other room then. (*Sits up a bit, sighs.*) It's an awfully long way, though.

ETHEL: You should be ashamed, a man your age. Why aren't you like my husband? Up at 6:30, mowing the lawn. . . .

GEORGE: The neighbors must hate him.

ETHEL (*Ignoring him*): . . . cleaning the yard, pruning trees . . . washing his car . . . then to work for a long, full day . . . home for dinner . . . then working in the basement . . . or repairing the roof . . . always working.

GEORGE: He'll kill himself some day. (*Pause*) Ethel, would you get me a glass of milk . . . and brush this fly off my nose?

ETHEL (*Exasperated*): This can't go on forever, George.

GEORGE: Sure it can. I collect unemployment insurance, sickness benefits because of my headaches. . . .

ETHEL: What headaches?

GEORGE: The ones I get when I don't collect my sickness benefits. Old Age Assistance.

ETHEL: Old Age? You're hardly thirty.

GEORGE: I asked them for an advance now and then—in case I didn't *reach* old age. (*Pause*) Would you mind tying my left shoelace? It feels loose.

ETHEL: You're impossible. A man who refuses to work.

GEORGE: I don't refuse to work. I'm just waiting for the right job.

ETHEL: For *ten* years?

GEORGE: It's not *my* fault. I'm here. All they have to do is come for me.

ETHEL: What kind of a job are you waiting for?

GEORGE: Oh, an inventor's job, for instance. I'm an inventor. I invented a machine where you turn a lot of knobs and music comes from far away.

142

ETHEL (*In despair*): That's a radio. That was invented before you were born.

GEORGE: Go ahead. Pick on me for things that happened before I was born. (*He yawns.*) I'm tired. I'd better go up to my room and take a nap. (*He goes out.* ETHEL *sits down angrily, sighs, bites her nails, then gets up and paces the room.*)

ETHEL (*To herself*): That brother just has to go. He's lazy, shiftless, and always in the way. I'll have Bill speak firmly to him right away. (*She goes out.*)

CURTAIN
* * * *

At this point, the curtain can come down, or be pulled across the stage, or the lights can dim. If a curtain or lights aren't available, a boy (or a girl, since they're nice, too) can say, "That's the end of the first scene. If you'll all shut your eyes and count to ten, an hour will have passed. I don't know why. It's the kind of thing that happens when you push the clock ahead for Daylight Saving Time."

Scene Two takes place in the living room, too. BILL, a neat young businessman, is sitting on the couch reading the paper. GEORGE comes in, yawns, sits down on the couch, and relaxes.

BILL (*Glaring at* GEORGE): Look, brother, my wife says it's time I spoke to you. What did you do today?

GEORGE: I took a bath.

BILL: That's all? You didn't go look for work?

GEORGE: When they want me, they'll send for me. I'm perfectly happy, waiting.

BILL: But I'm not, and my wife is not.

GEORGE (*Shrugs*): You know how it is with me and work. Too heavy for light work. Too light for heavy work. Most jobs are too dull. Others are too interesting—they raise my blood pressure. The ones in-between are too in-between. I have trouble working days because I take a nap in the morning and the afternoon. I can't work nights because that's when I sleep.

BILL: George, Ethel feels this house isn't big enough for all of us.

GEORGE: I'll be sorry to see her go.

BILL: *She* isn't going. It's *her* house. *You're* going.

GEORGE (*Wounded*): Then you lied to me. Ten years ago you asked me here for the weekend.

BILL: And you've stayed ten years.

GEORGE: Sure. But I remember clearly, when I started to go one day, you said, "Stay as long as you like."

BILL (*Wearily*): Oh, all right, we'll talk about it later. Look. My boss is coming here. Please try to be alert. And no stale jokes. My boss is a serious man. He's a great engineer and the head of my department.

GEORGE: I won't say a word. You know how *I* am.

BILL (*Nodding*): That's what worries me. (ETHEL *enters.*)

ETHEL: Couldn't you go out for a walk when Mr. Spiff comes, George?

GEORGE: I just took a bath. You want me to get pneumonia?

ETHEL: It's *hot* out.

GEORGE: You want me to get prickly heat?

BILL (*Irked*): Nobody ever died of prickly heat. Not yet.

GEORGE (*Wistfully*): Is that what you want? My picture in a medical textbook: "The first man ever to die of prickly heat"?

ETHEL: All right. Just don't butt in. (*Pause*) There's the bell. (*She goes off, comes back with* MR. SPIFF *who car-*

ries papers or a briefcase. BILL *gets up, shakes hands with* MR. SPIFF.)

BILL: Glad to see you, Mr. Spiff.

SPIFF: Hmmn. Yes. (*Stares at* GEORGE.)

BILL: This is brother George.

GEORGE (*Shakes hands without getting up*): Nice knowing you. Say, do you know the difference between a collision and an explosion?

SPIFF (*Turns nervously away from* GEORGE *and talks to* BILL, *pointing to papers, etc.*): Now, Bill, you'll notice here that the floor shift has been placed a little too much to the left, while the manifold. . . .

GEORGE: In a collision, you know where you *are*. But in an explosion, where *are* you? (*He laughs uproariously.* SPIFF *frowns.* ETHEL *makes motions over* SPIFF's *shoulder to* GEORGE. GEORGE *reacts dumbly, shrugging, staring behind him, looking puzzled, etc.*)

SPIFF: Now, in the automated section of the plant here . . . the memory banks will store transistorized knowledge of the input so that the assembly line will turn out these floor shifts.

GEORGE: Here's a hot one. A traveling salesman noticed a farmer feeding his hog with a teaspoon. The traveler said, "Won't it take a long time to fatten a hog that way?" The farmer said, "Sure, but what's time to a hog?" (GEORGE *laughs uproariously. He hits* SPIFF *on the back.* SPIFF *nearly collapses, but tries to ignore* GEORGE.)

SPIFF: Now, here is the completed model. You'll notice we've streamlined the body.

GEORGE: No sense of humor. (*He peers over* SPIFF's *shoulder at the plans.* ETHEL *again tries pantomime to suggest* GEORGE *go for a walk, go to bed, have a snack, etc. Once or twice,* SPIFF *catches her, and she turns her pantomime*

145

into smoothing her hair or doing setting-up exercises.
GEORGE *finally speaks to* SPIFF.) You forgot one big thing.
Women hate to back up in an automobile. They always
hit something. Right? Right. So lots of women won't buy
a car because they're scared to back up. (*Takes folded
paper from pocket and opens it*) I once had a girl who
used to pull up a little ahead of a parking space and ask
for help from pedestrians. The third time she did it, a
charming fellow backed the car right into the next state.

ETHEL: George—the—the geranium needs watering.

GEORGE: Huh? The geranium? It's plastic. (*He shows
paper to* SPIFF.) This is my design for a car with a steering wheel, brakes and headlights in back as well as in
front. A woman wants to back up she just gets in the rear
of the car and drives forward. Like the old-fashioned
trolley cars. They could be steered from either end.
You drove to the end of the line, and instead of turning
around, you went to the other end of the car and drove
from there.

SPIFF (*Looks over plans carefully, frowning, then slowly
smiling*): A splendid notion. Of course, it has bugs.

GEORGE: They can be smoothed out. If it works, we can sell
millions of cars to women who can't back up. We'll pre-
vent injuries to people they bump into. And trees. We'll
save a lot of trees.

SPIFF (*Shakes* GEORGE'S *hand*): I'm going right back to the
plant to study this. You never can tell, there may just be
a germ of something here.

GEORGE: I'll go with you. (*They both go out, excited.
ETHEL turns to BILL and throws up her hands in despair.
BILL sits down, in agony.*)

BILL: My great break. Spiff liked my plans. He was going
to promote me. Then that moron had to come up with

his crazy notion. Drive backwards! How about the rear seats? They'd have to face backwards. And what if someone grabbed the rear wheel and started driving backwards. . . .

ETHEL: Yes . . . while you were driving frontwards.

BILL: It's crazy. Ten years of this. Ten long, horrible years.

ETHEL: Ten weary, heart-breaking years.

BILL (*Vigorously*): I'd have taken him bodily and thrown him out long ago, if he wasn't your brother.

ETHEL (*Stands still for a moment, stunned*): My . . . *my* . . . brother? I always thought he was *your* brother! (*They stare at each other awhile.*)

THE END

THE EYES HAVE IT

This skit takes place in the examining room of an eye doctor. There should be a desk, a hat rack, a chair or two, and an eye chart that says:

GET YOUR

SPECTACLES

AT FINLAY

AND FINKELMANS
TEN YEARS TO
PAY

❖ ❖ ❖ ❖ ❖

Characters
THE DOCTOR
GEORGE FRUSH
NURSE ROCKY
A MAN

AT RISE: *The* DOCTOR *is sitting at his desk, eating a sandwich.* GEORGE FRUSH *enters. He is wearing thick glasses, and certainly doesn't see very well. But then, neither does the* DOCTOR. GEORGE *also has a sheepdog haircut, and this doesn't help.*

DOCTOR (*Looking up and smiling vaguely*): Good day, madam. You need glasses.
GEORGE: I'm George Frush.
DOCTOR: All right. Now, how many pairs of eyes does na-

ture give us? One. **Right.** We must guard our eyes carefully. Sit down. (*He takes a chair, places it near* GEORGE, *but not quite close enough.* GEORGE *sits down, but misses the chair.*) That's bad for your eyes. Shakes them to pieces. (GEORGE *feels around for chair, gets up.* DOCTOR *moves chair again.* GEORGE *sits and misses again.* DOCTOR *shakes his head.*) I warned you about that. (*Calls*) Oh, Nurse! Nursie! (*The* NURSE *comes in. She is obviously a boy with a deep voice, big feet, and big hands, dressed as a nurse.*)

NURSE: You called, Doctor?

DOCTOR: Yes. Help this man to a chair. He needs glasses. (NURSE *helps* GEORGE *to chair.*)

GEORGE: Who's that?

DOCTOR: My nurse. Mr. Frush, meet Nurse Rocky. (GEORGE *stands up, arm stretched out, ready to shake hands. He walks forward, bumps into hat rack, feels pole.*)

GEORGE: Nurse, you don't eat enough. You're skinny as a hat rack.

DOCTOR: No, no, my boy. Let me help you. (DOCTOR *gets up, takes* GEORGE *by arm. The two bump into desk, end up by hat rack again.* DOCTOR *feels hat rack.*) Nurse, you *are* losing weight. I'll say this, though: your muscles are firm.

NURSE (*Waving*): I'm over here. (*She runs over, shakes hands with* GEORGE, *leads him back to chair. The* DOCTOR *sits down behind the desk.*)

DOCTOR (*To* GEORGE): I should explain. I broke my own glasses this morning. I have an assistant coming in to help me. I called the doctor pool. This man is a stranger, so we must be patient with him. Meanwhile, George, read the chart.

149

GEORGE (*Looking at* NURSE): I don't see anything to read. I just see a big nose, a big mouth, a big jaw. . . .

DOCTOR: You're looking at the nurse. Look at the chart.

GEORGE: Where is it?

NURSE: He can't even see the *chart!*

DOCTOR: He needs glasses. (*To* GEORGE, *as he points to chart.*) Over there, George.

GEORGE (*Squinting*): Oh. It says . . . uh . . . Exit to Coffee Shop and Parking Lot.

DOCTOR: You remember that from someplace else. Now read the chart. (*Pointing*) It's hanging right up there.

GEORGE (*Looking around*): Where?

DOCTOR: I don't know. I told you I broke my glasses. (*He gets up and starts looking for the chart.* GEORGE *gets up, too. They bump into each other.*) Who's that?

GEORGE: It's your patient.

DOCTOR: Well, sit somewhere or we'll keep bumping into each other. (GEORGE *sits down on* NURSE, *who is sitting in a chair.*)

NURSE: Ouch! You're sitting on me.

GEORGE (*Getting up quickly*): *I* wondered why the cushions felt so hard. They're your knees.

DOCTOR (*Bumps into hat rack and stares at it*): I thought I told you to sit down. (*Picks up hat rack and tries to push it down.*) Your joints are pretty stiff, aren't they?

NURSE: Doctor, you're pushing the hat rack. (GEORGE *has found the chart. He feels it and stares at it closely.*)

GEORGE: I found the chart!

DOCTOR: Good! Read it.

GEORGE (*Nose on chart*): A . . . E . . . I . . . O . . . U . . . and sometimes W . . . and Y.

DOCTOR: Is that right, Nurse?

NURSE: Not exactly.

GEORGE: I'll try again. (*Backs away a little.*) A . . . B . . . C . . . D . . . The doctor here gives Green Stamps free.

DOCTOR (*Shaking his head*): You're not even close. I think you need *two* pairs of glasses. You're myopic with a touch of spondulix in the east ventricle, plus, I believe, a shortsighted case of stripped gears in your flywheels. What do you think, Nurse?

NURSE (*Shaking head*): I don't think anything. I didn't get paid this week yet.

DOCTOR: As soon as my helper gets here, we'll test his carburetor. I think the points need cleaning. (*At this point, a* MAN *walks in, carrying a black bag.*) Ah, Doctor!

MAN: I'm not a doctor.

DOCTOR: I know. But you soon will be. Patience. That's what makes doctors. Take care of George. I think he needs glasses.

MAN (*Looks at* NURSE): Did you pick out this nurse?

DOCTOR: I did.

MAN: I guess I know who needs glasses.

DOCTOR: Nurse, you may go. (NURSE *goes out, making a face at* MAN.) She may not look like much, but you should see her kick field goals.

MAN: Look, I came here . . .

DOCTOR: Take care of this boy. That's all I ask. I insist.

MAN (*Shrugs. Takes plunger, snake and other plumbing equipment out of bag. Puts plunger to* GEORGE's *heart.*). Hmmmn. Sounds like clogged pipes.

DOCTOR (*Makes a note*): Always a factor.

MAN (*Sends metal snake down* GEORGE's *coat and out again*): At least his drain isn't stopped up.

DOCTOR: Good. No sinus trouble. (*Makes a note.*)

GEORGE (*Giggles*): It tickles.

DOCTOR: It doesn't hurt, though.

MAN (*Takes flashlight and looks down* GEORGE's *throat, holding plunger menacingly in other hand*): How long is it since you had new faucets?

GEORGE: Quite a while, I guess.

MAN: Hmmmnnn. . . . (*Looks in* GEORGE's *ears, feels the back of his neck. Gets in front of* GEORGE *and pulls on his jacket like a tailor. Backs away, stares. Grabs some of the seat of* GEORGE's *pants.*) It might help you if I let out the jacket a little and took in the seat of the pants. I think there is a pressure created.

DOCTOR: What I thought. Pressure on the eyeballs.

MAN: I could weld everything up with a blowtorch.

GEORGE: What?

DOCTOR: I don't think we have to be so drastic. What medical school did you go to?

MAN: No medical school. I tried to tell you—I'm a plumber. And that will be fifteen dollars, even.

GEORGE: A plumber!

DOCTOR: Send me a bill.

GEORGE (*Disgusted*): A plumber!

DOCTOR: O.K. Fix the faucets in the other room. (MAN *goes out.* GEORGE *starts for the wall.*)

GEORGE: I'm leaving. (*He bumps into wall.*)

DOCTOR: Wait a minute. (*Walks to* GEORGE. *They bump into each other.*) Excuse me, George. (GEORGE *moves aside and walks into hat rack.*)

GEORGE: Pardon me, Doctor. (DOCTOR *moves and takes hold of hat rack.*)

DOCTOR: Now listen to me, George. (GEORGE *goes to desk, grabs rubber glove, shakes it.*)

GEORGE: Good-bye, Doctor. (*The glove sticks in his hand. He tries to shake it off.*) What have I done!

NURSE (*Entering*): Everything all right?

GEORGE (*Waving glove*): The doctor's hand came off.

NURSE: You need glasses. That's a rubber glove. (NURSE, *annoyed, pushes* GEORGE's *hair. This brushes it out of his eyes. He looks around joyfully.*)

GEORGE: I can see!

NURSE (*Handing glasses to* DOCTOR): Doctor, I found your glasses. (DOCTOR *puts glasses on.*)

DOCTOR: I've been eating too much spinach. Everything looks green.

NURSE: You have your sunglasses on.

GEORGE (*Dancing around*): I can see. I can see! I don't need glasses. (*Pushes hair away from face.*) I need a haircut. (*He starts to go. The* DOCTOR *and the* NURSE *grab him.*)

DOCTOR: In the next room. I'll cut your hair.

GEORGE (*Struggling*): I thought you were a doctor.

DOCTOR: When things get dull, I also cut hair. (*The* DOCTOR *and* NURSE *pull* GEORGE *off.*)

THE END

GREAT CAESAR!

The setting of this skit is a public place in Rome. It must be Rome because a sign tacked up says: ROME.

❖ ❖ ❖ ❖ ❖

Characters
JULIUS CAESAR
BRUTUS
SOOTHSAYER
CASSIUS
MARK ANTONY
CALPURNIA

AT RISE: CAESAR *and* BRUTUS, *dressed in togas, are walking along.*

BRUTUS: That's a pretty classy toga you're wearing, Caesar.

CAESAR (*Fingering toga*): A man in my position has to look smart. Actually, Calpurnia took it in a bit. I've lost weight—no starches, easy on the sugar, and a little exercise raising a Roman standard fifteen times every morning.

BRUTUS: This is the fifth spring for my toga. It's an all-season, Dacron and cotton.

SOOTHSAYER (*Offstage*): Caesar! Yoo-hoooooo!

CAESAR: Who is it that calls on me? Speak! Caesar is turned to hear.

BRUTUS: That's the kind of talk I hated in high school.

154

(*The* SOOTHSAYER *appears. She is witch-like and carries a sign:* SOOTHSAYING AT ALL HOURS. FORTUNES TOLD. SPELLS CAST. WE GIVE PLAID TRADING STAMPS. WIN A FREE CHARIOT.)

SOOTHSAYER: Beware the ides of March!

BRUTUS: A soothsayer, Caesar, bids you beware the ides of March.

SOOTHSAYER: Beware the ides of March.

CAESAR (*To* BRUTUS): This dame bugs me, verily.

BRUTUS: Scram, soothsayer! You bug noble Caesar.

SOOTHSAYER: O.K. Don't say I didn't warn you clowns. (*Goes out.*)

CAESAR (*Shrugging*): Some kind of nut.

BRUTUS (*Nodding*): The lunatic fringe. Hippies.

CAESAR: She has a voice like my mother-in-law. (*He starts out.*) Farewell. I must go to write a speech.

BRUTUS (*He raises his hand high but his toga starts to slip so he tucks it back in one way or another.*): Hail, noble Caesar. All Gaul is divided into three parts!

CAESAR: I'll see you around the campus. (CAESAR *goes.* CASSIUS *enters.*)

BRUTUS: Cassius, I thought you were in training.

CASSIUS: I'm the greatest. Who needs to train? I'm the most beautiful, too.

BRUTUS: I like modesty in a man. Verily.

CASSIUS (*Hand to ear*): Hark! (*Shouts are heard from off-stage.*)

BRUTUS: Mantle hit a home run, I'll bet.

CASSIUS: Nay. The people are offering immortal Caesar a crown. The people want Caesar for their king! Did he ever lick anyone? (*More shouting offstage.*)

BRUTUS: Maybe Yogi Berra hit a home run.

CASSIUS: No. More honors for Caesar.

Why should that name be sounded more than yours?
Write them together, yours is as fair a name;
Sound them, it doth become the mouth as well;
Weigh them, it is as heavy. (*Pauses, smiles proudly, speaks in an aside to audience.*) Shakespeare. Act I, Scene 2.

BRUTUS: I'll think it over. My girl says I'd make as good a king as Caesar. Of course, Caesar is a nice guy.

CASSIUS: He's for the birds. A big show-off.

BRUTUS: In a straight election, he couldn't carry Ward Six, that's true. But he's a big shot on the battlefield.

CASSIUS: Malarkey. He takes all the credit for your bravery.

BRUTUS: By Jove, 'tis true. Caesar must bleed. Gentle friend, let's kill him boldly, but not wrathfully. (*To audience*) Also Shakespeare. (MARK ANTONY *enters.*)

BRUTUS: Ho, Mark Antony! Ho, ho!

CASSIUS: A Caesar stooge. A ward-heeler!

BRUTUS (*His hand on* MARK ANTONY'*s shoulder*): I thought you were going around with Cleopatra.

MARK ANTONY: By Jove, I'm in the wrong play. (*He exits.*)

CASSIUS: That guy's a fink. (*The two go off.*)

CURTAIN
* * * *

Sometimes it is wise to have a Director or Stage Manager. This gives someone a part that he can ad lib for laughs or play straight. Right here, for instance, the Stage Manager could pretend to be drawing the curtains together (they may even stick) or down. He can say, "That is the end of the first scene. The next scene is in Caesar's home. Miss McMurphy, our teacher here, you'll have to imagine is a marble fountain, and Charlie Brown, in the front row, is the viaduct. Caesar and his wife Calpurnia are talking things over."

CALPURNIA: Don't go anywhere for a few days, Julius. I had a nightmare last night. I dreamed they were bumping you off.

CAESAR: Calpurnia, my dear wife, you had too much fried pigeon and deep dish apple pie last night. That pie is *rich*.

CALPURNIA: Nay. Stay home for a few days. We'll have fun with Scrabble.

CAESAR: You just want to keep me home. You're jealous.

CALPURNIA: Great Caesar. My dream was clear. Brutus killed you.

CAESAR: Brutus is my friend. Forget the whole thing. If they make me king, I'll make him tax-collector. That's where all the money is.

CALPURNIA: I beseech you. It thunders and lightens . . . or lightnings, or whatever it is.

CAESAR: What you need is a new hat, and a few new togas. I understand plaid is big this year. Get a plaid toga.

CALPURNIA: I warn you, Julie!

SOOTHSAYER (*Singing from offstage*):
> Double, double, toil and trouble
> Fire burn, and cauldron bubble
> Mix it with a baboon's blood
> Then the charm is warm and good.
> Cool it, man,
> Cool it, man,
> Let it bubble in your soul,
> That's the ole witches' rock and roll.

CAESAR: What's that? It sounds like "Macbeth."

CALPURNIA: I left the radio on. It's a new group from Carthage.

CAESAR: Give me the old tunes like "Sweet Sue" and "Night and Day." (*He sings his favorite songs and dances around.*)

CURTAIN
* * * *

Scene Three takes place on a street. CAESAR *enters with* CASSIUS, MARK ANTONY, BRUTUS, *and perhaps some others.*

CAESAR: The ides of March hath come.

BRUTUS: They sure hath, Caesar, old pal.

CASSIUS: And how! (CASSIUS *feels the edge of a knife.*)

CAESAR (*Looking at knife*): What's that?

CASSIUS: Oh, a little knife my wife asked me to have sharpened.

CAESAR: I wish you'd put it away. It makes me nervous. (BRUTUS *takes out a knife and feels it.*) You, too, Brutus?

BRUTUS: I was going to peel an apple later.

CAESAR: I wish you fellows would lay off. I'm worn out from learning the Limbo from Calpurnia. (*Pause*) I wanted to make a speech. Romans, Cassius sayeth he is the greatest but I am the greatest. I am the living most. I am unassailable. I am constant and true as the Northern Star. Yon Cassius sayeth he is the prettiest but simple truth bids me say, verily I am the prettiest and the bravest and the strongest. And any of ye guys who get wise will end up on the trash heap of history. Right, Mark Antony?

MARK ANTONY: Why don't we all go and see Cleopatra? It's only ninety-nine cents before noon.

CASSIUS: Hail, Caesar! Great Caesar! (*He stabs* CAESAR.)
CAESAR: Careful with that thing. Ugh! You could hurt
somebody.
BRUTUS: Caesar, you talk too much. (*Puts the finishing
touches on.*)
CAESAR: Brutus, you fink! (*He falls as if dead.*)

CURTAIN
* * * *

Scene Four takes place on the same street. MARK ANTONY
—and others— enter, carrying CAESAR's body (it is dressed
in fancy pajamas). CASSIUS, BRUTUS, and CALPURNIA enter.
The body is put down, and CALPURNIA goes over to it.

CALPURNIA: Doesn't he look handsome? I made those pajamas for him. (*Cries are heard from offstage.*)
MARK ANTONY: The people are aroused.
BRUTUS: Why not? The World Series starts tomorrow.
CASSIUS: I like the Yankees, myself.
BRUTUS: Excuse me. I have to make a eulogy. (*Speaking
toward audience.*) Fellows, you all thought Caesar was a
great guy. So did I. If you want to know why I bumped
him off, I'll tell you. Not that I loved Caesar less but that
I loved Rome more. I mean, where are the sewers we
need? The four-lane chariot ways? The new municipal
stadium? What about the World's Fair Caesar turned
down? It would have brought in a lot of hotel and night
club business. I liked Caesar. Personally, we got along
well. But Rome comes first, and Caesar was no good for
Rome. An egghead. Not practical. Look at the down-
town area and the vacant stores. No parking facilities.
I mean, fellows, Caesar had to go. (*Moment's silence.*)

O.K., Mark. I mean, if you can forget about Cleopatra for a minute, it's your turn.

MARK ANTONY: Friends, Romans, countrymen, lend me your ears. (I need a new writer.) Caesar did not want to run Rome. The people asked him three times; three times he said he wasn't a candidate. He meant it. Caesar was the greatest. He was noble, handsome, kind, generous, brave, true, faithful . . . uh . . . intelligent . . . the noblest Roman of them all. He never did one wrong thing. He was kind to animals and a member of the Safety Patrol. (CAESAR *gets up and turns over. Everybody backs away.*)

BRUTUS: What was that?

CAESAR (*Sticking his head up*): I was just turning over in my grave.

THE END

GOOD MORNING, YOUR HONOR

The setting is a courtroom. If possible there should be a raised bench for the Judge. If not, a table will do. There should also be some chairs. The Judge should have a robe. It can be makeshift and ill-fitting—something tent-like and too long that covers him up and over which he can easily trip.

❖ ❖ ❖ ❖ ❖

Characters

POLICEMAN
HENRY SMITH, *an inoffensive parking violator*
JUDGE
MRS. HENRY SMITH, *Henry's wife, a formidable woman*
VIOLA GOOBER, *a female lawyer, and public defender*

AT RISE: *There is a POLICEMAN beside the bench. Standing before the bench is HENRY, a meek-looking, pleasant man, the defendant. Slightly away from the rest is a woman, VIOLA, in severe, tailored clothes and flat shoes. She is an attorney, the public defender. MRS. HENRY SMITH, a firm, determined woman, is near her husband (HENRY). The JUDGE is not present when the scene starts.*

POLICEMAN (*Banging a stick on the floor as he cries*): Court! (*Anyone who is seated stands. The* JUDGE *comes in from the side, smiling and nodding, tripping over his robe, getting it caught here and there, finally getting it twisted around his leg or his shoe. He gets it unwound, with dignity. He sits down, picks up gavel.*)

JUDGE (*Striking gavel down on his other hand*): Ouch! (*He opens a book.*)

POLICEMAN: Henry Smith, charged with illegal parking. (HENRY, *pushed by his wife, steps forward.*)

JUDGE: Henry Smith, you are charged with the serious and solemn matter of illegal parking. How plead you?

HENRY: How plead I?

JUDGE: How do you plead?

HENRY: Guilty, Your Honor.

JUDGE: Guilty? That's no fun.

HENRY (*Pounding bench*): But I *was* guilty. (HENRY *keeps his hand on bench.*)

MRS. SMITH: I don't think you were, if you want my opinion.

HENRY: Sh-h-h.

JUDGE: Who's that? (*He bangs gavel. This time on* HENRY's *hand.*)

HENRY (*Holding hand, in pain*): My wife.

JUDGE: I could have guessed it.

MRS. SMITH: If you want my opinion, I . . .

JUDGE: The court does not want your opinion.

MRS. SMITH: You'll get it, anyway. The city makes up big fancy parking spaces for big shots, but the people, where can they park? Two dollars an hour someplace?

HENRY: This was a meter.

MRS. SMITH: You shut up.

JUDGE (*To* MRS. SMITH, *pointing gavel*): *You* shut up. You

162

are making accusations of bribery and so on. To make criminal charges *is* a criminal charge.

HENRY: Look, I plead guilty. I did it.

MRS. SMITH: You didn't do anything. Big shots, like judges, have a space with their name on it. They park there. Small people . . . they find a space, they stop . . . they steer and wiggle . . . and somebody else beats them to it. Not judges, they have a big space, big enough for a limousine. And how do they get the limousine? Not on their salaries, believe me. (JUDGE *bangs gavel on his hand again*.)

JUDGE: Mrs. Smith, I will hold you in contempt.

MRS SMITH: Go ahead. You hold me in contempt. I'll hold you in contempt.

HENRY: Please, my dear. I plead guilty.

JUDGE: I want you to know your rights in spite of your wife. You are entitled to legal counsel under a ruling of the Supreme Court, Fitzpatrick vs. the State of Wyoming, 102-345 Zip Code 01108. This counsel will gladly be supplied by the court, free.

VIOLA (*Stepping forward*): I am Attorney Viola Goober. I will defend you. Your Honor, this man is a victim of circumstance. Brought up an orphan, he was forced to go to work in a pretzel factory at the age of six. . . .

HENRY: Look, I don't need a lawyer. The fine for parking is two dollars. I am guilty. Any way you look at it. I parked illegally. I want to pay the fine and go back to work.

JUDGE: The court feels you are entitled to a fair and honest hearing. This court is precise and correct in every respect. Neatness counts here.

MRS. SMITH: Anyway, he couldn't see the parking meter because he forgot his glasses.

HENRY: Sh-h-h.

JUDGE: Forgot your glasses, huh? How could you see to drive?

MRS. SMITH: And what's more, he was in a hurry. He was late for work. Otherwise he would never have come down Fort Pleasant Avenue at seventy miles an hour. It certainly scared me.

JUDGE: Seventy miles an hour, huh?

HENRY (*Very nervously*): Please, Your Honor. I plead guilty to the parking offense. The case is closed.

JUDGE (*Banging the gavel on* HENRY's *head*): Oh, no, it isn't.

VIOLA: Your Honor, because of the complications of the case, I move for a jury trial.

JUDGE: That I'd like. I get lonesome all by myself.

HENRY: I don't want a jury trial. I'm guilty. Fine me the two dollars. I'm a nervous wreck.

MRS. SMITH: I should think he would be. Seventy miles an hour with *our* brakes. If you can call them brakes. (HENRY *gasps.*)

VIOLA: I think my client should be excused. According to Statute 7798, Section 6687, Paragraph 5576, Clause 3, a man cannot be held on a parking violation if he doesn't even have a driver's license.

JUDGE (*Banging gavel on his own hand*): Ouch! No driver's license, eh? This is getting more and more serious.

HENRY: Of course, I have a driver's license, Your Honor. It's just that I couldn't find it, when Miss Goober here asked to see it. You see I've been very nervous lately. My car looks something like the getaway car in the Finks Million Dollar Bank Robbery. (JUDGE *almost falls off the bench.*)

JUDGE: The getaway car! The million dollar robbery!

164

VIOLA: Your Honor, I ask that the defendant be released on $50,000 bail so that a case can be prepared to prove his innocence in the million dollar robbery.

HENRY (*Weakly*): I wasn't *in* any robbery. I wasn't doing anything. I was just parking illegally because the meter wouldn't take my nickel. I pushed and pushed. I banged and banged . . . Then I went into the bank for change. The Finks Bank.

JUDGE: The Finks Bank! It certainly looks bad. The getaway car. The speeding. The meek, innocent look of the defendant. An obvious character to front for bank robbers. Would they have a criminal type fronting for them? Would they have a thug for a lookout? Who would they pick if they wanted a meek, timid, faceless milksop?

MRS. SMITH: My husband.

HENRY (*Almost in tears*): I am guilty of parking illegally. The nickel wouldn't fit. I went into the bank . . . the lines were so long I couldn't wait . . .

JUDGE: It just doesn't make sense. Can you prove it?

VIOLA: Your Honor, this is terribly serious. My client is a victim of circumstance. He is badly in debt. The payments on the TV and the convertible bed are coming up. He needs money desperately. He is approached by criminal characters. Although he is innocent at heart, having been well-trained in honor, he is tempted. His share of a million dollars would make him a new man . . . no longer would he have to listen to his boss shout at him . . . no longer would he spend sleepless nights worrying about his bills . . . he could take a trip to Paris . . . meet some beautiful girls. . . .

MRS. SMITH (*Hitting him*): You rascal! (JUDGE *hits* MRS. SMITH *with gavel.*)

VIOLA: His share of a million was . . . what?

JUDGE: Well, Henry, what was it?

HENRY: All I did was park illegally. Fine me the two dollars, *please.*

VIOLA: Let us say it was a mere $100,000.

MRS. SMITH: What did you do with it, Henry?

JUDGE: Yes. Where is it? Make restitution and ten years could be cut off your sentence.

HENRY (*Almost fainting*): It's just a parking ticket. (*Holding up ticket.*) It says here . . . look . . . two dollars' fine . . . appear in court and pay the two dollars and . . .

MRS. SMITH: So you were planning to leave your loving wife, your wife who is always tender and warm-hearted, who has worked her fingers to the bone for you, who . . .

JUDGE: Don't forget, "has given the best years of her life to you."

MRS. SMITH: Thank you. Who has given the best years of her life to you. Planning to skip to Paris with a hundred thousand dollars—

HENRY: All I did was park illegally.

VIOLA: I must ask that my client be tried before a jury . . .

JUDGE: Well, this court *is* neat and orderly and wants everything done correctly.

HENRY: I don't want a jury trial.

JUDGE: Very well, he waives his right to a jury. It is now the duty of the court in this case—and I haven't had such a peachy one in a dog's age—imagine! A million dollar bank robbery! In view of the *habeas corpus,* the *rigor mortis,* the *corpus habeas,* the writ of *mandamus,* the *spiritus frumenti,* the *omnia Gallia* and the *e pluri-*

bus unum, I sentence you to five to ten years in the State Prison at Dingle Dell. Take him away! (HENRY *barely keeps from fainting by clutching the bench. The* JUDGE *bangs the gavel on* HENRY's *hand, and he slips to the floor. The* POLICEMAN *helps him up.*)

POLICEMAN: Do you play baseball? They need a shortstop at the State Pen.

HENRY: Your Honor . . .

JUDGE: The case is closed. This has worn me out. You can't imagine how nerve-wracking these things can be.

VIOLA (*To* HENRY): This is wonderful.

HENRY: W-w-wonderful?

VIOLA (*Joyfully*): We'll appeal! We'll take it to the highest court in the land! You'll become a famous crook. Oh, this is a big day in my life! And how proud you'll be, Mrs. Smith! Your husband's picture in all the papers . . . with *you* as the little woman who is waiting faithfully for him.

JUDGE (*Dreamily*): The little woman to whom he owes everything. (MRS. SMITH *beams.*)

VIOLA: You'll probably be on TV quiz shows, soap commercials—maybe even a Senate investigation.

MRS. SMITH: I've always wanted to see the cherry trees in Washington.

HENRY (*Gasping*): Judge, I am innocent.

JUDGE: You said you were guilty.

HENRY: I'm guilty, but I'm innocent.

JUDGE: All right, I'll be big-hearted. I'll release you on $50,000 bail.

HENRY: Where would I get it?

JUDGE: Out of the hundred thousand you stole.

HENRY: All I did . . . there was this parking meter. . . . I had a nickel . . . this parking meter . . . the nickel

. . . I found a parking ticket . . . this nickel . . . this meter . . . I . . .

JUDGE: The case is closed.

POLICEMAN (*Banging stick*): Court is adjourned.

JUDGE (*Rising*): That's what I like. A day in court where everything is neat and in its place. Where everything is just and precise, nothing forgotten, no loose ends, nothing untidy. (*He steps down from bench, starts to exit, and trips on his robe. He stands up, and as he does so, his robe opens, revealing that he has forgotten his trousers. He is wearing shorts with red hearts on them and garish red, white, and blue socks. Unaware of his odd costume, the* JUDGE *strides pompously across the stage and exits. Curtain.*)

THE END

THE CAREFREE HIGH SCHOOL ORCHESTRA

This little sketch is about a school orchestra. Everybody has played in, or been forced to listen to, a school orchestra. Everyone always feels proud, too, even when it hurts. The time is morning assembly at Carefree High School; the setting, the stage of the auditorium. There are chairs on-stage for the orchestra.

❖ ❖ ❖ ❖ ❖

Characters

ARMAND, *a temperamental music teacher, who conducts the orchestra, and looks like a conductor. He has wild hair, and a baton.*

HARRY
BRENDA
ESTHER
PHIL } *members of the orchestra*
BILLY
JOE
OTHER PLAYERS

AT RISE: *The members of the orchestra—or at least nine or ten of them—are in place in their chairs. They should pretend to have musical instruments—violins, trumpets, drums, harps . . . anything. ARMAND is standing near them. He smiles broadly at the audience, looks around at orchestra, taps his baton, and frowns. The members of the orchestra continue to chat with each other, laughing, etc. They ignore* ARMAND.

ARMAND: Order, please! (*He turns back to audience and then around again.*) Is missing, someone?

HARRY: Billy, the drummer.

ARMAND: With him I will deal when he arrives. (*To the audience*) Young men and ladies, teachers and guests. This morning, at assembly, we reap the real fruits of months of work with the Carefree High School Orchestra. When I was brought here from New York to be in the music department, I spoke with many students to make an orchestra. I saw it was hopeless. So, this morning we are going to play the first movement of Beethoven's Second Symphony.

BRENDA: I was out sick. Can you tell me how it goes?

ARMAND: Certainly. (*He hums a jazzy popular tune*)

BRENDA: Thank you. I thought that was Bach. (*She pretends to play on a violin.* ARMAND *winces, and turns to the audience.*)

ARMAND: We are all amateurs here, and you must not expect too much.

ESTHER: A good joke always makes things easier. I had to shoot my dog yesterday.

ARMAND: Was he mad?

ESTHER: He wasn't exactly pleased. (*Everyone laughs, including* ARMAND, *who then shifts quickly back to his professional attitude.*)

ARMAND: Boys and girls. teachers . . . Beethoven's Second Symphony. Many of my fine musicians . . . if I may exaggerate . . . have early classes so we will take just a minute while I tell you what to listen for in this great work and then we will begin to play. The Second Symphony comes after the First and before the Third.

PHIL: It comes right in the middle of the First and Third.

ESTHER: Is this the second movement of the First Symphony or the first movement of the Second Symphony?

ARMAND: A good question. Now, in this magnificent work . . . (BILLY, *the drummer, has dashed in. He sits down. He pretends to be taking some hot breaks on the drum.* ARMAND *turns around.*)

BILLY: Hi, professor. What's cooking?

ARMAND: You are late.

BILLY: I forgot my drumsticks. I went home, but I didn't have my house key. I rang the doorbell. My mother stuck her head out the window and said, "Billy's not home." So I said, "All right, I'll come back when he is."

ARMAND: Very logical.

JOE (*To* BILLY): How do you use the word archaic in a sentence?

BILLY: Archaic? We can't have archaic and eat it, too. (*They all laugh.* ARMAND *calls for attention.* BILLY *beats up a storm on the drum, then stops.*)

ARMAND: *Please!* Time is passing swiftly. We must *play*. (*To audience*) In the opening passage of this beautiful work you will hear the violin. It is a theme of love and vengeance. The gypsies are singing gaily on their way to the fair. Upstairs in a huge castle, Lucy de Lima is sad. This is stated by the trumpet. She is about to marry the Duke of Glutz . . . stated by the bass violin. All the peasants are coming to the wedding. Each one is bringing an ox. Then we have a long, beautiful solo which suggests that Rudolph, unknown to Lucy, is really the murderer . . . it was *not* the butler, this time. By chance . . . and you will hear the clarinet brood over this . . . the Duke of Glutz, who is really a gypsy impostor . . . finds a blood-stained ski sweater which he turns over to his mother, one of the Beverly Hillbillies in disguise. Now. . . .

ESTHER (*To* JOE): I spent the weekend at the Cape. We stayed at The Green Star. The food was poison.

JOE: That's too bad.

ESTHER: And such small portions, *too*. (*They all laugh.* ARMAND *calls for order.*)

ARMAND: The Duke, seeing Lucy from afar, eating artificial roses, orders the arrest of the gypsy king, who is, really, the district attorney in disguise. Everyone is invited to a banquet and poisoned. You will hear this as a low, moaning melody by the full orchestra. After this comes a delicate harp interlude which was inserted by a friend of Beethoven's named Peanuts, who wanted to give the thing a little lift. It conveys gently the idea of Lucy thinking of the loneliness of her life and stabbing the gypsy king in the back.

PHIL: He stole that from Brahms.

ARMAND (*Glares at* PHIL, *turns back*): At this point is a most exquisite clarinet solo that requires a master. It suggests the pain Lucy endures from eating lobster stuffed with shrimp in bed the previous night. For this fine part of the symphony we have Joe. Joe!

JOE (*Stepping forward*): I didn't learn it.

ARMAND: You saw long ago my notice on the bulletin board. "Wanted: a boy who plays clarinet exquisitely; a boy of dependability, courage and strength; a boy high in his marks; a boy who is not nervous, a boy I could trust."

JOE: I'm not strong. I have no courage. My marks are low. I'm very nervous. And I can't play the clarinet.

ARMAND: Then why did you come to me?

JOE: I wanted you to know that on *me* you should not depend. (*He goes back and sits down.*)

ARMAND: Well, at least he is honest. (*Taps his baton*) Now, ladies and gentlemen, teachers, parents . . . we are ready for the great moment. (HARRY *walks up to him, whispers in his ear.* ARMAND *nods and* HARRY *goes off.* ARMAND *explains to audience.*) Harry has an early class in botany. Now, we begin. . . . (BRENDA *goes to* ARMAND *and whispers to him.* ARMAND *shows annoyance but nods.* BRENDA *goes out.*) She has to do research on tadpoles right away. Now . . . let us commence this great musical treat . . . (*Raises baton.* ESTHER *comes to him and whispers. They pretend to argue in soft tones.* ESTHER *leaves. The other members of the orchestra who do not have speaking parts come to* ARMAND *and chatter. After a moment, they go out.*) The wrestling team and the girls' basketball team practice at nine-thirty. Ah, well . . . now, we will have the great, melodic music of the master of them all. . . . we will play for you, my patient audience. (JOE, BILLY, *and* PHIL *come and whisper to* ARMAND. *There is some discussion, but the boys go out.*) A pity, indeed. They have a class immediately in Roman history. But now . . . *really* . . . we will play for you . . . (*Raises baton, looks around, sees no one there*) At last, you will hear the beautiful first movement from Beethoven's Second Symphony. (ARMAND *mimics a violin and then other instruments, jumping around, conducting himself, changing tones*) Eeeee . . . EEEEEEE . . . aaahh. Boom,

boom, boom. Ta-da. Ta-ta-ra-ta-ta-ta. Baw . . . dum
. . . dee-dee. CRASH! Tra-la-la-la-la-la-LA. . . . CRASH!
BOOM-BOOM! Teedle-dee-deedle-dee. Mmmmmmm-
mmmmmmm, tra La . . . tee-dee. BOOM! CRASH-
CRASH. (*He continues a wild, maniacal singing, humming, crashing, and conducting until—*)

THE END

EMERGENCY

This is a short skit about an emergency, hence the title. It shows how the medical profession is on its toes, and the patients are on the beds. It takes place in the living room of the Fuzzys.

❖ ❖ ❖ ❖ ❖

Characters
JIM FUZZY, *a husband. You know.*
DR. GLUTTON, *a doctor*
DR. SOCKEM, *another doctor*
DR. QUINCE, *a third*

AT RISE: JIM *is on the telephone.*

JIM: Hello, Dr. Glutton? . . . Hello? Doctor, it's an emergency. What? . . . No, it's not a body job. It's not an engine job, either. . . . What? Oh, the West Side Garage! Excuse me. . . . I'm so nervous. In fact, I'm shaking. I ought to take my tonic because it says to shake well before I take it. (*Hangs up, dials again*) Hello? . . . What? The operator? I dialed 114-739-7-4-Rh-SOS-1234, who are we for? Yes. . . . That number is not a working number? Well, give me one that is. It's an emergency. I want Dr. Glutton, of Glutton, Sockem and Quince on Firglade Avenue, upstairs over the candy store. Yes, I'll dial it again. . . . My poor wife! What? No, she isn't in any pain. She's in bed sick, that's all.

. . . What? I don't want another wife. I want a doctor. I'll dial again. (*Hangs up, dials again*) Hello? This is an emergency. *Hello?* What? (*Repeats slowly*) Clearing and cooler in western New England today, followed by tomorrow. But. . . . what? You *said* that. (*Hangs up, dials again*) Hello, Dr. Glutton? Jim Fuzzy. . . . It's an emergency. My wife is very sick. She has spots before her eyes and spots in back of her. . . . You'll hurry? What? You use radio-directed cars? You'll be here immediately. Good. (*He hangs up. Three doctors walk in the door,* GLUTTON, SOCKEM *and* QUINCE. *They carry black bags.*)

GLUTTON: At ease, men.

JIM: That was fast, doctor.

SOCKEM: In an emergency, we work like lightning.

QUINCE: We're there in a flash, if you're paying in cash.

GLUTTON: I'll do the talking. (*To* JIM) What seems to be the matter with your wife?

JIM: She gets a sinking feeling in bed.

SOCKEM: It could be livid pectorises from eating the skins of prickly pears.

GLUTTON: Quiet, I'll do the talking.

JIM: Why do you need three doctors?

GLUTTON: I am a specialist, Sockem is a general practitioner, and Quince drives the car and makes wonderful melted cheese sandwiches.

QUINCE: I was very popular for that at medical school.

JIM: Look, Dr. Glutton, my wife is ill. There is no time to waste.

GLUTTON: Be calm. Leave it to Glutton, Sockem and Quince. If it can be cured, we'll cure it. If it can't be cured, you shouldn't have it.

JIM: Please check her, doctor. (GLUTTON *goes off.*)

QUINCE: Don't worry, Mr. Fuzzy. We've taken care of

some tough cases. The last place we were, we cured a man of shingles and then repaired a leaky faucet.

SOCKEM: The place before that, we cured a man's mother *and* his race horse. It was two-for-one day, *plus* free medicine up until four o'clock.

GLUTTON (*Comes in*): I'll need a saw. (SOCKEM *opens a bag and gives him a saw.* GLUTTON *goes back.*)

JIM: That sounds bad.

SOCKEM: Glutton's a great saw man.

GLUTTON (*Back again*): I'll need some copper pipe. (SOCKEM *takes it out of a bag.* GLUTTON *takes pipe, goes out. Sounds of banging are soon heard from offstage.*)

QUINCE: Don't worry, Mr. Fuzzy. Lots of people need the old lead pipes replaced with copper ones.

JIM: What's he doing? He's banging and sawing her! (*Starts off. Other doctors restrain him.*)

SOCKEM: Don't worry. Glutton knows his business. He's maybe testing her reflexes.

QUINCE: Or waking her up. (GLUTTON *comes in again.*)

GLUTTON: I'll need a blow torch, a crowbar and a screwdriver. (SOCKEM *takes them out of bag.* GLUTTON *goes back.*)

JIM: This is terrible! What is he *doing* to my wife?

QUINCE: Have faith in Glutton. He's an all-around specialist. He's never lost a patient yet unless she skipped town.

SOCKEM: He may be replacing her gall bladder with an aluminum siding. It's quite the thing.

QUINCE: It may be nothing more than cleaning her oil filter.

JIM: I can't stand this! Give me something, doctor. (SOCKEM *takes a small mallet out and hits him on the head.* JIM *falls gently and slowly into a chair, smiling.*)

SOCKEM: That's the *single* dose.

177

JIM: That's enough.

QUINCE: Remember the fellow we had to give the *triple* dose to?

SOCKEM: Broke my best hammer.

GLUTTON (*Coming out with tools, smiling*): It's all fixed. I had quite a job. Sawing, welding, hammering. But she's going to be all right.

JIM: Oh, thank you, doctor!

GLUTTON: Yes, the front legs of the bed were too short. That's why she had that sinking feeling. I had to lengthen the legs. (*He starts out.*)

QUINCE (*Looking at a piece of paper*): We have a woman who swallowed a nut and bolt on Cherryvale Avenue.

GLUTTON: Be sure we have a screwdriver. (*To* JIM) That'll be fifteen dollars. Ten dollars for the call and five for repairs to furniture and fixtures. (JIM *gives him some money.* GLUTTON *starts out with* QUINCE *and* SOCKEM. SOCKEM *turns back, pulls stamps out of bag, gives them to* JIM.)

SOCKEM: Double green stamps today.

THE END

UNITED SPIES

If this is not the way international spies operate, it is pretty close. The setting is the headquarters of United Spies Exchange in a nameless city in a mysterious country. (Where else?) There is a desk, and a sign that says: UNITED SPIES. WE ARE EVERYWHERE AT ONCE AND THAT'S NOT EASY. *There may be other signs:* WATCH YOUR HAT, COAT AND MILITARY PLANS . . . ALWAYS LOOK BEHIND YOU. . . . FALSE BEARDS AND WIGS FOR RENT . . . *etc. Every spy in this little demonstration should have papers and plans sticking out of his or her pockets. There is no end to the disguises the spies can use, but only a few wigs and beards are really necessary.*

❖ ❖ ❖ ❖ ❖

Characters

GUMBAL RO, *president of United Spies*

VLADIMIR KOZ, *a Mulvanian spy, crooked*

IRMA LAFLAMME, *a beautiful spy, but also crooked*

HANS GUTTEL, *another spy, crooked as a pretzel*

JACK, *a Transylvanian spy, honest and trustworthy*

At Rise: Gumbal Ro *is sitting at his desk.* Vladimir Koz *comes in.*

Koz: Good evening, Mr. Ro, president of United Spies. I have information for sale or exchange.

Ro: Good. You are a loyal union member, Koz.

Koz: I have the *exact* menu our premier eats for breakfast every Sunday.

Ro: Good. Anything else?

Koz: I have the plans for a new moon capsule Mulvania is planning.

Ro (*Shrugs*): So? There is a glut of moon capsules. Every country has a moon capsule. There is not much of a market for moon capsules.

Koz: I am doing my best. I am trying to earn money to find my long-lost mother.

Ro: A spy who cannot find his mother is not much of a spy. (Koz *looks under table, up to ceiling, in closet, etc.*)

Koz: Mama, Mama, where are you? (Irma LaFlamme *enters. She is a beautiful-type spy who rolls her eyes and looks mysterious. As she passes* Koz, *she swipes a plan from his pocket, but this is all right because he has swiped one from her trenchcoat.* Koz *runs to* Irma.) Do you have long golden curls and the smell of peppermint Life-Savers on your breath?

Irma (*Aghast*): But no! I have, on my breath, soup de jour, and on my head, short black hair.

Koz (*Hopefully*): Maybe you left your golden curls at home? (*Pause*) Oh, Mama, how I miss you! Mama, Mama. Your long golden curls . . . oh, Mama.

Irma: I, Irma LaFlamme, Europe's most beautiful spy, have the plans for Ali Ben Mustapha's new tennis court.

Koz: I will trade you a Mulvanian moon capsule and two photographs of Princess Rosalind in a bathing suit.

Irma: I will trade you one secret treaty between Mona Lisa and Julius Caesar for a piece of apple pie with strong cheese.

Ro (*Laughs*): Who can obtain so valuable an item? (Hans Guttel *enters, clicks his heels, bows to everyone.* Irma *and* Koz *pick papers from* Hans' *pocket, but when he gets straightened out he takes other papers from their pockets.*)

Hans: I, Hans Guttel, the world's most handsome and admired spy, have for sale the complete plans of Sultana to revolt.

Ro: Against whom?

Hans: Against the East Sultana Sauerkraut Makers. The stuff is getting terrible.

Koz: I'll give you General Tamara's recipe for chocolate brownies for it.

Hans: I need cash. Since I met Greta I can't eat, I can't sleep, I can't do anything.

Ro: Why?

Hans: I'm broke!

Koz (*Scornfully*): In Mulvania, a spy never falls in love. (*To* Hans) Have you seen my beloved mother anywhere? She was a tall short woman with a slim fat figure . . . a petite Roman nose and a false red beard.

Hans (*Thoughtfully*): I saw a false red beard in Ochtenberg last Tuesday, but nobody was in it.

Koz: You don't know what it is to look for your mother! Oh, Mama, Mama!

Ro (*Looking around at all of them*): I can get you all a lot of money for answers to these questions: What is the exact number of intercontinental fruit pies Transylvania has?

Koz: I don't know.

Ro: What is Transylvania's precise plan for cheese fondue?

Irma: I don't know.

Ro: How fast is Transylvania's fastest practical toaster?

Hans: I don't know.

Ro (*Sarcastically*): I hope you don't mind my asking you these questions.

Koz: Not at all. If you don't ask questions you'll never learn anything. (Jack, *a Transylvanian spy, enters. He is well-dressed but obviously a woman in men's clothes. He wears a big brimmed hat or a top hat. At the sight of him,* Irma, Hans *and* Koz *hook on false beards hastily.*)

Jack (*His voice breaks every now and then*): Sorry I'm late, pals. I knew it was the important weekly exchange of information, but I was busy stealing Ochtenberg's plan to attack Camelot.

Ro: There is no Camelot.

Jack: That's why they feel they can attack it. They also have plans to attack Babylon, Nineveh and several American stagecoaches. I am willing to sell the plans for a million dollars. (*He picks something from* Hans' *pocket.* Hans *retaliates.* Irma *gets it from* Hans. Koz *picks it from* Irma. Jack *steals it back from* Koz)

Hans: I'll give you two dollars and a half.

Jack: For two dollars and a half I will give you Wolfe's plan to take Quebec from Montcalm.

Hans: It's a deal. (*Hands over money*)

Jack (*Hands over a plan*): You also get a coupon worth fifty cents toward the purchase of six cakes of violet soap.

Koz: Soap! Ha, ha! Who needs soap?

Ro (*To* Jack): In all the time you have belonged to the United Spies, you have never exchanged anything valuable.

Jack: Why should I? I am not really a spy. I am a member of the Intelligence Service.

Irma: That's better?

Jack: It sounds better. Besides I am loyal to Transylvania, my adopted homeland. How I love the national anthem. "Oh, Transylvania, oh, Transylvania, tra, la, la. . . ."

Irma: It does not thrill me as much as to hear the pheasants coming down the side of the mountains singing *The Mayonnaise!*

Ro (*To* Jack): You say you are loyal to Transylvania. This is very unfair.

Hans: *Not* the thing.

Irma: Very rude these days. We spies must be one for all and all for one.

Koz: We must be internationally-minded or we will never be friends.

Hans: Besides, if we conceal things from each other, one of us might have to go to work.

Ro: A decent international spy, with any honor or decency, will bring us the information we need just as we will bring him . . . or her.

Hans: Yah!

Irma: Ah!

Koz: Dah!

Jack: Bah! (*Goes and pulls their false beards*) You see, you are not even on the level with *me*. (*The telephone rings, or* Ro *pretends it is ringing, and picks it up. While he is talking,* Koz *is walking closer to* Jack *and eying him sharply.*)

Ro (*On the phone*): Hello? What? Yes, this is United Spies. What? It's incredible! Is there no honor among people today? Is there no common decency? Eh? Yes. Yes. Terrible! Sickening. (*He hangs up. To others*) We must get out of here. We are not safe. This is heartbreaking. (*Pause*) Someone is spying on us! (*All but* Koz *and* Jack *gasp. They are too busy staring at each other.* Koz *finally tears off* Jack's *hat and long golden curls fall down.*)

Koz: Mama! Mama! (*They embrace, not forgetting to pick each other's pockets. While* Koz *and* Jack *embrace, the others do a little dance around in a circle, picking pockets and having their pockets picked.*)

THE END